GALÁPAGOS ISLANDS

a different view

Georgia Purdom, *General Editor*

First printing: September 2013

Master Books® is a division of the New Leaf Publishing Group, Inc.

ISBN: 978-0-89051-781-9
Library of Congress Number: 2013944452

Cover & interior design by Diana Bogardus

Unless otherwise noted, Scripture quotations are from the
New King James Version of the Bible.

Please consider requesting that a copy of this
volume be purchased by your local library system.

Printed in China

Please visit our website for other great titles:
www.masterbooks.net

For information regarding author interviews,
please contact the publicity department at (870) 438-5288

Master Books®
A Division of New Leaf Publishing Group
www.masterbooks.net

TABLE OF CONTENTS

ACKNOWLEDGMENTS — 3

INTRODUCTION — 4

BEGINNINGS — 8

STONES AND STARS — 12

CLIMATE, CURRENTS, AND COLONIZATION — 24

LIFE AND LEGACY — 42

FLORA AND FAUNA — 60

REFLECTIONS ON THE GALÁPAGOS — 86

CONCLUSION — 92

ABOUT THE AUTHORS — 96

REFERENCES — 100

Sally Lightfoot crab

ACKNOWLEDGMENTS

This book would not have been possible without the assistance and dedication of many writers, reviewers, and editors. I had a vision for what I wanted this book to be, and they helped make it a reality. Thank you to all the authors who have very busy personal and professional lives but took time out of their schedule to write a portion of this book.

Thank you to Danny Faulkner, Tom Hennigan, Jean Lightner, Tommy Mitchell, Terry Mortenson, Michael Oard, Ron Samec, Frank Sherwin, Andrew Snelling, Larry Vardiman, Gordon Wilson, and John Whitmore who dedicated time and effort to reviewing sections of this book. A special thank you to Tom Hennigan, a fellow traveler to the Galápagos Islands, for his insights and wisdom in writing, reviewing, and planning this book. A special thank you as well to Andrew Snelling for his encouragement and assistance in putting together this book.

Thank you to Roger Patterson and Stacia McKeever for their reviewing and editing skills. They helped make what we wrote more readable, understandable, and grammatically proper. What would I do without you!

A special thank you to Lance and Penney Davis of Living Science in Atlanta, Georgia. I am grateful for your adventurous spirit and for asking me to go on the trip of a lifetime. I greatly appreciate your passion for teaching students the truth of God's Word through science.

Thank you to Master Books and Laura Welch for their commitment to and enthusiasm for this book. Their skills and effort made this book spectacular.

Thank you to my husband, Chris, and daughter, Elizabeth. They encouraged me to go to the Galápagos Islands even though it meant two weeks away from them. I am especially proud of my brave little girl, whom I know missed me dearly. A special thank you to my mother-in-law, Sylvia, who gave up two weeks of her life to help take care of my family.

Most of all, thank you God for Your mercy and majesty that is clearly exhibited in the Galápagos Islands and for Your Son Jesus Christ who saves us.

3

An aura of mystery surrounds the Galápagos Islands, located off the coast of Ecuador in the Pacific Ocean. How were they formed? Why are so many species of animals found only on these islands? Why do they play such a prominent role in the debate over origins?

Over the years, scientists and theologians alike have visited this archipelago that spans the equator, seeking to find answers to these questions. One of the most famous visitors was Charles Darwin, a naturalist aboard the ship the HMS *Beagle* in 1835. While in the Galápagos for several weeks, he observed a wide variety of animals — large tortoises, marine iguanas, blue-footed boobies, and, perhaps the most famous of them all, finches.

The differences he saw among living creatures — tortoises with different shell shapes, finches with a variety of beak shapes, iguanas with very different eating behaviors (and other observations and influences apart from the Galápagos) — eventually led Darwin to propose the idea that all living things descended from a common ancestor over millions of years. He believed that the small differences in living creatures that he observed could over time result in large differences that would change one kind of organism into a different organism.

Yet, with a better understanding of what the Bible teaches, Darwin could have arrived at a much different — and true — conclusion about the past history of the Galápagos Islands.

4

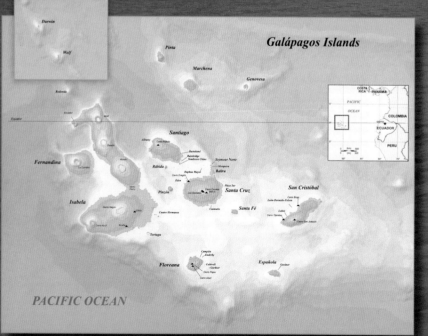

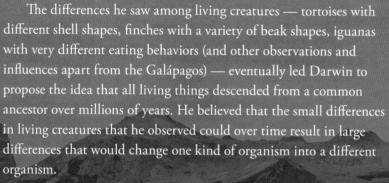

A BIBLICAL PERSPECTIVE ON THE GALÁPAGOS

But now ask the beasts, and they will teach you; and the birds of the air, and they will tell you; or speak to the earth, and it will teach you; and the fish of the sea will explain to you. Who among all these does not know that the hand of the LORD has done this, in whose hand is the life of every living thing, and the breath of all mankind?

— Job 12:7–10

The Galápagos Islands are truly a living testament to these verses in Job. The wildlife of the Galápagos displays both the majesty of God's creation and His mercy in preserving life in a cursed world.

In Genesis 1 we read that God created everything by His spoken command in six days. The Hebrew word for *day* used throughout Genesis 1 should be understood as a literal 24-hour day, since it is used with the words morning, evening, and a number (for example, "So the evening and the morning were the first day" [Genesis 1:5]). And calculations from father-son genealogies given in Genesis 5 and 11 and elsewhere in Scripture give us a date for creation that is approximately 4,000 years before Jesus came to earth (or roughly 6,000 years before today).

Genesis 1 also reveals that God created plants and animals according to their kind (Genesis 1:12, 21, 24–25). The inference from Scripture (Genesis 1 and 6–8) is that plants and animals were to reproduce according to their kinds. The word *kind* most likely correlates to the family level in modern classification schemes. One basis for this determination is that most animals within today's "family" can breed with one another and produce offspring (e.g., a zebra and donkey can mate and produce a zonkey).

The mistake made in Darwin's day (and before) was teaching that this meant God created each species of today's animals in the spot where they're found today. A better understanding is that, in the beginning, God created a wide variety of animal and plant kinds and from these have descended the various species. Further, today's animals have migrated to their respective habitats over the past few thousand years and were not created *in situ*. The teaching from Genesis is clear that one kind of plant or animal did not evolve into a

Nazca boobies

different kind over millions of years.

Thus, the finches Darwin observed are descendants of the original kinds and have adapted (via mutations, natural selection, mediated design, and other mechanisms) to their present environment over the past few thousand years. Scientific studies show that this type of change and speciation can happen very quickly (on the order of tens or hundreds of years, not millions). And scientific studies have also shown that mechanisms such as mutation and natural selection actually work against molecules-to-man evolution (the type proposed by Darwin).

Everything God originally created was "very good" (Genesis 1:31). There was no disease or death. And God gave all animals and humans plants to eat — carnivory was not present in the very beginning (Genesis 1:29–30). There was no fear between man and animals or between various kinds of animals. We see echoes of this in the Galápagos Islands with the animals who have no fear of humans.

Then Adam disobeyed God's command (sinned) and God's decreed punishment for sin was death (Genesis 2:16–17, 3:6, 3:19; Romans 5:12). God placed a curse on His beloved creation (Genesis 3:14, 3:16–19; Romans 8:22). This event introduced death, disease, and suffering into God's once-good creation. And this is the reason the echoes of Eden seen in the Galápagos are marred. We no longer live in a "very good" world. If Darwin had kept this event in mind, it would have reshaped how he viewed God and His creation.

Galápagos finch

Adam and Eve's children and grandchildren continued to disobey God's command. In Genesis 6–8 we read of God's judgment on sin in the form of a catastrophic global Flood about 4,500 years ago. The tectonic upheaval associated with the "fountains of the great deep" (Genesis 7:11) eventually resulted in the formation of the Galápagos Islands.

God mercifully saved Noah, his family, and representatives of all air-breathing, land-dwelling animal kinds on the ark. After the floodwaters subsided and the ark landed, the animals began migrating over the globe via land bridges, rafting, and other means. Some of the Galápagos animals appear to have migrated to the islands from the mainland of South America. God designed organisms with the ability to adapt in the new and different world (caused by both the Fall and the Flood) and this is clearly seen in the Galápagos flora and fauna.

THE PLACE OF SCIENCE

But how do we know that this account of the formation and colonization of the islands is true? These events happened in the past and, therefore, fall into the category of historical (or origins) science. Historical science encompasses past events that we cannot observe, test, or repeat.

When people use the term *science,* they are usually referring to observational (or operational) science. This is science that happens in the "here and now." We can observe, test, and repeat it. Scientists use it to develop computers, vaccines, and airplanes. It is very different from historical science that tries to understand events that have occurred in the past. Observational science is not as dependent on the scientist's worldview. Historical science—encompassing origins, events from the past, and the age of the earth—is dependent on the scientist's worldview. All scientists look at the same evidence when it comes to the past — the same rocks, the same fossils, the same islands, and the same animals. The difference is in their starting point.

Many reject the God-inspired biblical accounts of past events, such as creation, the Fall, and the Flood because they prefer instead the ideas that humans have come up with based on their own reasoning.

Galápagos dove

Since we were not eyewitnesses of the past, we must rely on outside help to understand the past. Many will use expressions like "science says," or "the evidence says," to support their ideas about the past. But evidence such as rocks and fossils doesn't speak. Instead, scientists are the ones doing the speaking, and their interpretation of past events is always based on their starting point, or worldview. Do they start with man's ideas apart from God or do they start with God's Word?

The scientists and theologians in this book interpret evidence based on the worldview that the Bible is the history book of the universe and inerrant in its original form. God begins His record of history in the Bible when time begins (Genesis 1:1), and since God is the author (2 Timothy 3:16; 2 Peter 1:21) and cannot lie (Titus 1:2), we can only have an accurate account of the past when we start with God's Word. Likewise, when we look at events that are not directly recorded in Scripture, we can only develop an accurate understanding of the past when we base our thinking on God's Word.

DOES IT MATTER WHAT I BELIEVE ABOUT THE HISTORY OF THE GALÁPAGOS?

The problem that arises when secularists and even some Christians deny the history presented in Genesis is the undermining of the authority of Scripture. If one part of the biblical record is wrong, then it is possible other parts are wrong, too. Many Christians accept the virgin birth and Resurrection of Jesus Christ, yet question the Genesis account of creation. Many will say that science proves the earth is old and evolution has occurred. The problem with this appeal to "science" is the impact it has on their other beliefs related to Scripture. "Science" has clearly shown that virgins don't give birth and people don't come back to life after being dead for three days. These Christians are

Waved albatross

inconsistent not only in what miracles of God they choose to believe but also in their definition of the word *science*.

Even though the formation of the Galápagos Islands and its colonization by plants and animals occurred in the past, we can still use observational science to study it today. We can observe how recent volcanic activity is changing the islands. We can observe how animals are continuing to change. Catastrophic events like volcanic eruptions change the landscape in a short period of time. Millions of years are not required. Mutations, natural selection, and other mechanisms cannot change animals and plants from one kind into a completely different kind. Evolution from a single common ancestor is not true. What we understand from historical science, beginning our thinking with a biblical starting point, is actually confirmed by the findings of observational science.

Ultimately a choice has to be made: do we put our faith in man's ideas about the past or in God's Word? I hope that this book will help you see the Galápagos Islands from a different view — a biblical view. I pray that the choice will be clear and that you will learn to trust the Creator of the heavens and the earth and His Word, the Bible.

CREATION (GENESIS 1:1–2:3)

In the beginning God created the heavens and the earth. The earth was without form, and void; and darkness was on the face of the deep. And the Spirit of God was hovering over the face of the waters.

Then God said, "Let there be light"; and there was light. And God saw the light, that it was good . . . God called the light Day, and the darkness He called Night. So the evening and the morning were the first day.

Then God said, "Let there be a firmament in the midst of the waters, and let it divide the waters from the waters." . . . And God called the firmament Heaven. So the evening and the morning were the second day.

Then God said, "Let the waters under the heavens be gathered together into one place, and let the dry land appear"; and it was so. And God called the dry land Earth, and the gathering together of the waters He called Seas. And God saw that it was good.

Then God said, "Let the earth bring forth grass, the herb that yields seed, and the fruit tree that yields fruit according to its kind, whose seed is in itself, on the earth"; and it was so. And the earth brought forth grass, the herb that yields seed according to its kind, and the tree that yields fruit, whose seed is in itself according to its kind. And God saw that it was good. So the evening and the morning were the third day.

Then God said, "Let there be lights in the firmament of the heavens . . ." and it was so. Then God made two great lights: the greater light to rule the day, and the lesser light to rule the night. He made the stars also . . . And God saw that it was good. So the evening and the morning were the fourth day.

Then God said, "Let the waters abound with an abundance of living creatures, and let birds fly above the earth across the face of the firmament of the heavens." So God created great sea creatures and every living thing that moves, with which the waters abounded, according to their kind, and every winged bird according to its kind. And God saw that it was good. And God blessed them, saying, "Be fruitful and multiply, and fill the waters in the seas, and let birds multiply on the earth." So the evening and the morning were the fifth day.

Then God said, "Let the earth bring forth the living creature according to its kind: cattle and creeping thing and beast of the earth, each according to its kind"; and it was so. And God made the beast of the earth according to its kind, cattle according to its kind, and everything that creeps on the earth according to its kind. And God saw that it was good.

Then God said, "Let Us make man in Our image, according to Our likeness; let them have dominion over the fish of the sea, over the birds of the air, and over the cattle, over all the earth and over every creeping thing that creeps on the earth." So God created man in His own image; in the image of God He created him; male and female He created them. Then God blessed them, and God said to them, "Be fruitful and multiply; fill the earth and subdue it. . . .

And God said, "See, I have given you every herb that yields seed which is on the face of all the earth, and every tree whose fruit yields seed; to you it shall be for food. Also, to every beast of the earth, to every bird of the air, and to everything that creeps on the earth, in which there is life, I have given every green herb for food"; and it was so. Then God saw everything that He had made, and indeed it was very good. So the evening and the morning were the sixth day.

Thus the heavens and the earth, and all the host of them, were finished. . . . and He rested on the seventh day from all His work which He had done.

THE FALL (Genesis 2:15–3:19)

Then the LORD God took the man and put him in the garden of Eden to tend and keep it. And the LORD God commanded the man, saying, "Of every tree of the garden you may freely eat; but of the tree of the knowledge of good and evil you shall not eat, for in the day that you eat of it you shall surely die." . . .

And the LORD God caused a deep sleep to fall on Adam, and he slept; and He took one of his ribs, and closed up the flesh in its place. Then the rib which the LORD God had taken from man He made into a woman, and He brought her to the man. . . .

Then the serpent said to the woman, "You will not surely die. For God knows that in the day you eat of it your eyes will be opened, and you will be like God, knowing good and evil."

So when the woman saw that the tree was good for food, that it was pleasant to the eyes, and a tree desirable to make one wise, she took of its fruit and ate. She also gave to her husband with her, and he ate. Then the eyes of both of them were opened, . . .

So the LORD God said to the serpent:

"Because you have done this, you are cursed more than all cattle, and more than every beast of the field; on your belly you shall go, and you shall eat dust all the days of your life.

And I will put enmity between you and the woman, and between your seed and her Seed; He shall bruise your head, and you shall bruise His heel."

To the woman He said:

"I will greatly multiply your sorrow and your conception; in pain you shall bring forth children; your desire shall be for your husband, and he shall rule over you."

Then to Adam He said . . . "Cursed is the ground for your sake; in toil you shall eat of it all the days of your life. Both thorns and thistles it shall bring forth for you, and you shall eat the herb of the field. In the sweat of your face you shall eat bread till you return to the ground, for out of it you were taken; for dust you are, and to dust you shall return."

9

Death came as a result of sin

THE FLOOD (GENESIS 6:5–9:16)

Then the LORD saw that the wickedness of man was great in the earth, and that every intent of the thoughts of his heart was only evil continually. And the LORD was sorry that He had made man on the earth, . . . So the LORD said, "I will destroy man whom I have created from the face of the earth, both man and beast, creeping thing and birds of the air, for I am sorry that I have made them." But Noah found grace in the eyes of the LORD. . . .

And God said to Noah. . . . "Make yourself an ark. . . . The length of the ark shall be three hundred cubits [450 feet], its width fifty cubits [75 feet], and its height thirty cubits [45 feet]. . . . And behold, I Myself am bringing floodwaters on the earth, to destroy from under heaven all flesh in which is the breath of life; everything that is on the earth shall die. But I will establish My covenant with you; and you shall go into the ark — you, your sons, your wife, and your sons' wives with you. And of every living thing of all flesh you shall bring two of every sort into the ark, to keep them alive with you; they shall be male and female. Of the birds after their kind, of animals after their kind, and of every creeping thing of the earth after its kind, two of every kind will come to you to keep them alive. . . .

Thus Noah did; according to all that God commanded him, so he did. . . .

So Noah, with his sons, his wife, and his sons' wives, went into the ark because of the waters of the flood. Of clean animals, of animals that are unclean, of birds, and of everything that creeps on the earth, two by two they went into the ark to Noah, male and female, as God had commanded Noah. And it came to pass after seven days that the waters of the flood were on the earth. . . . all the fountains of the great deep were broken up, and the windows of heaven were opened. And the rain was on the earth forty days and forty nights. . . .

He cuts out channels in the rocks, and his eye sees every precious thing.

—Job 28:10

And the waters prevailed exceedingly on the earth, and all the high hills under the whole heaven were covered. . . . And all flesh died that moved on the earth: birds and cattle and beasts and every creeping thing that creeps on the earth, and every man. All in whose nostrils was the breath of the spirit of life, all that was on the dry land, died. . . . Only Noah and those who were with him in the ark remained alive. . . .

Then God remembered Noah, and every living thing, and all the animals that were with him in the ark. And God made a wind to pass over the earth, and the waters subsided. The fountains of the deep and the windows of heaven were also stopped, and the rain from heaven was restrained. And the waters receded continually from the earth. . . . Then the ark rested in the seventh month, the seventeenth day of the month, on the mountains of Ararat. . . .

And it came to pass . . . in the first month, the first day of the month, that the waters were dried up from the earth. . . . And in the second month, on the twenty-seventh day of the month, the earth was dried.

Then God spoke to Noah, saying, "Go out of the ark, you and your wife, and your sons and your sons' wives with you. Bring out

with you every living thing of all flesh that is with you . . . so that they may abound on the earth, and be fruitful and multiply on the earth." . . .

Then Noah built an altar to the LORD. . . . Then the LORD said in His heart, "I will never again curse the ground for man's sake, although the imagination of man's heart is evil from his youth; nor will I again destroy every living thing as I have done. . . .

Then God spoke to Noah and to his sons with him, saying: "And as for Me, behold, I establish My covenant with you and with your descendants after you, and with every living creature that is with you. . . . Never again shall all flesh be cut off by the waters of the flood; never again shall there be a flood to destroy the earth."

And God said: "This is the sign of the covenant which I make between Me and you, and every living creature that is with you . . . I set My rainbow in the cloud, and it shall be for the sign of the covenant between Me and the earth. . . . The rainbow shall be in the cloud, and I will look on it to remember the everlasting covenant between God and every living creature of all flesh that is on the earth."

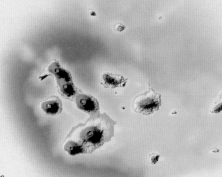

The Galápagos Islands are a chain of islands crossing the equator about 600 miles off the coast of Ecuador. The islands are exclusively the result of volcanic activity. As ocean-floor plates move over stationary "hot spots" in the earth's mantle, volcanoes form first underwater and eventually build to the point where they are visible above the water. The formation of these islands has been likened to a conveyor belt carrying the Nazca plate that is part of the earth's crust eastward over a hot spot. This results in the oldest islands being farther to the east (closest to mainland South America) and the newest islands to the west.

When I visited the Galápagos Islands, I was amazed at the great diversity of landscapes — from lush vegetation on the oldest islands to nearly barren lava fields on the youngest islands. On Isabela and Fernandina (the youngest of the islands) we viewed many prominent and still-active volcanoes. On some of the younger islands like Bartolomé, we saw the landscape dotted with numerous parasitic cones (the result of side eruptions). The combination of looming volcanoes, parasitic cones, and large black lava fields made you feel as if you were on another planet!

On Santiago, a "middle-aged" island, we hiked across a very large lava field, the result of an eruption just over a hundred years ago. The lava flowed for three months and was seven feet deep. Today, the field covers 15 square miles. It takes a boat moving along the coastline two hours to completely survey this lava field from the water! But even amid the seeming harshness of this landscape, we observed beauty and life — beauty in the amazing shapes formed as the pahoehoe lava flowed to form its smooth ropes and life in pioneer plants like mollugo, tiquilia, and lava cacti that conquered the bleak landscape.

On older islands, evidence of past volcanic activity is not as obvious. Española, the oldest island, is covered in lush vegetation such that it was hard for us to imagine volcanic eruptions ever took place there. However, when we viewed the black volcanic rocks composing steep cliffs on the coasts of the island we were vividly reminded of its origins. Another old island, Floreana, had over 50 small "hills," each the result of previous volcanic activity but now flourishing with vegetation.

We saw the beauty of God's creation not only on the land but also in the sky. The majority of the Galápagos Islands are not inhabited and light pollution is minimal. As a result, the view of the evening sky was breathtaking! The sentence "He made the stars also" in Genesis 1:16, telling of God's creation of the stars, doesn't seem adequate to express the beauty of the night sky. The Milky Way was clearly seen along with objects only seen in the Southern Hemisphere like the Southern Cross, the globular cluster Omega Centauri, and the Small and Large Magellanic Clouds.

Both secular and creation scientists can observe and study the land and sky of the Galápagos in the present. This falls under the category of observational science. But developing models for understanding how the islands formed in the past or how starlight reached earth rapidly in the past falls under

He gathers the waters of the sea together as a heap; He lays up the deep in storehouses.

—Psalm 33:7

13

the category of historical science. This type of science is greatly dependent on the scientists' worldview. Do the scientists start with man's ideas apart from God or do they start with God's Word?

Secular geologists believe the Galápagos Islands formed slowly over millions of years. They begin their studies with the belief that the present is the key to the past and that the slow geological processes we observe today were happening at the same rate in the past. Interpreting the evidence from this starting point, a view known as uniformitarianism, they conclude that the islands must have taken millions of years to form. Likewise, secular astronomers, operating from similar uniformitarian beliefs, think that light from objects, like the stars that compose the Small Magellanic Cloud, took around 200,000 years to reach earth.

Creation geologists believe the Galápagos Islands formed rapidly over hundreds of years. They start with God's Word and understand that past geological processes were greatly impacted by Noah's Flood. Rapid and catastrophic changes occurred in a short period of time, resulting in the formation of the islands in only a few hundred years. Biblical creationists reject uniformitarianism because of the presence of supernatural events revealed in the Bible — especially the creation week and the Flood. Creation astronomers believe that the light from stars was visible on earth from the fourth day of creation only about 6,000 years ago (Genesis 1:14–18). The rocks and the stars — the evidence — studied by all scientists, are the same; the only difference is the starting point or worldview of the scientist.

Many secular scientists believe radiometric dating proves that the islands are millions of years old. However, radiometric dating is based on assumptions about the past. If the scientists weren't

▲ Parasitic cones on Bartolomé

▼ Hills are dormant volcanoes on Floreana

there to observe the past, how do they know their assumptions about the past are accurate? Radiometric dating has been shown many, many times to give outrageously incorrect dates for rocks of known ages (like rocks from modern volcanic eruptions). According to these faulty dating results and because of the many unknown factors involved, the assumptions the scientists are using are wrong and radiometric dating does not prove the islands are millions of years old.

In Psalm 24:1–2, David says, "The earth is the LORD's, and all its fullness, the world and those who dwell therein. For He has founded it upon the seas, and established it upon the waters." And in Psalm 19:1 he says, "The heavens declare the glory of God; and the firmament shows His handiwork." The rocks of the Galápagos and the stars above it truly declare both the majesty and mercy of God. The earth and universe that God created can only be rightly understood when we look to His Word, which as David declares in Psalm 19:7, is "perfect."

▾ Volcano on Fernandina

▲ Marine Iguanas

▲ La Cumbre volcano, Fernandina
Photographed from the International
Space Station.

◄ Volcanoes on Isabela and Fernandia

THE GALÁPAGOS ISLANDS began as a group of underwater volcanoes that grew progressively from the ocean bottom until they finally emerged above sea level. Today there are 13 large islands, 6 small islands, and 42 islets all located near the equator in the Pacific Ocean about 600 miles west of Ecuador. Each island consists of a single volcano, except for Isabela, which consists of an overlapping string of six volcanoes.

The underwater volcanoes that became the Galápagos Islands are the result of a blob of hot rock that rose beneath this region during the latter stages of the Genesis Flood. As the blob came to within about 150 miles of the surface it began to undergo partial melting and generate basaltic magma. This magma was able to penetrate through cracks in the plate above it, pour out profusely onto the ocean floor, and form rapidly growing volcanoes.

What caused the rising blob? It was a response to the catastrophically rapid plate motions that occurred during the Genesis Flood. These rapid plate motions transferred the entirety of the pre-Flood ocean floor, in conveyor-belt-like fashion, into the earth's mantle. The rapid surface motions of the plates in the eastern Pacific region produced a rising plume that brought hot upper mantle rock close to the surface. The partial melting of this hot rock produced the magma and volcanism that formed the Galápagos Islands. Based on relative radioisotope dates, the Galápagos volcanism began near the end of the Flood. It continued at high volume for several centuries. The volcanism continues today, although at a much reduced level.

The Galápagos Archipelago, as it is called, is a chain of islands. Active volcanoes currently exist on the northwestern end of the chain, while the volcanoes on the southeastern end are completely dormant. This is not the result of motion of the plume, but rather southeastward movement of the Nazca Plate on which the islands ride over the plume. Today the rate of plate movement is only about three inches per year. However, at the end of the Flood cataclysm, the rate was much higher, on the order of a mile per year. The islands on the southeastern end of the chain, such as Española, formed first while they were located directly over the plume. As the Nazca Plate moved southeastward and these islands were transported away from the plume center, their volcanism diminished and eventually ceased. New islands formed to the northwest of the older ones as magma from the plume continued to find cracks in the plate it could penetrate.

Today the islands of Fernandina and Isabela on the northwest end of the chain now lie above the plume. These islands are the youngest and the most volcanically active, with more than 50 eruptions in the last 200 years. Although plate movement and island formation are relatively slow processes in the present, the catastrophic changes associated with the Flood caused rapid plate movements and formation of the islands in the past. The Bible's record of the past is an important starting point for a correct understanding of how the Galápagos Islands were formed.

JOHN BAUMGARDNER

VOLCANIC LANDSCAPES ARE some of the most unsettled places on the earth's surface. Not only do eruptions spew large volumes of ash and lava, they are responsible for dislodging huge masses of rock that can drastically alter landscapes within minutes.

The Galápagos are completely of volcanic origin, growing from the ocean floor after Noah's Flood (they have no fossil-bearing Flood sediments on them). There is currently not much rainfall in the Galápagos, nor are there many rivers to deeply erode the islands; so island geography must be completely explained by volcanism.

The Galápagos Islands are on the Nazca Plate that is moving southeast, toward the coast of Ecuador. The southeastern-most islands are smaller and lower in elevation, while the northwestern-most islands (where the active volcanoes are) are larger and higher in elevation. Farther to the southeast, there are numerous seamounts on the ocean floor — extinct volcanoes that never grew high enough to make it above sea level. Molten rock is generated in the earth's mantle under the Galápagos Islands, below the moving plate in a "hot spot." Over time, the hot spot doesn't move, but the plate does, producing a long chain of volcanoes building up on the ocean floor as the plate moves over the top of it. Currently, the hot spot is below the northwestern islands, causing the active volcanoes in that area.

During Noah's Flood the earth's plates moved rapidly (feet per second), and then they slowed to today's rates (inches per year). This explains the size pattern we see in the Galápagos Islands. The first volcanoes to build up on the seafloor were the seamounts toward the southeast. The plate was moving more quickly then, so those volcanoes never made it above sea level. As plate velocity slowed, the volcanoes grew larger and taller. That is why the biggest and highest islands, and the active volcanoes, are on the northwestern edge of the island chain — those islands have been sitting over the hot spot longer.

The Galápagos soils form as volcanic rock is chemically decomposed and then combined with organic debris from decaying plants. Soil formation is highly dependent on annual precipitation because moisture is necessary to alter the rock. Since many places in the Galápagos have near-desert conditions, soils are often thin or nonexistent. Many of the small islands are characterized by bare volcanic rock surfaces. Today, ocean waters off the coast of the Galápagos are cool and do not evaporate very well, resulting in the low annual rainfall totals. As the smaller islands were first starting to form after the Flood, ocean conditions were probably quite a bit warmer, leading to more rainfall, rapid rates of erosion, and faster rates of soil formation than what we see today. By the time the larger islands began to form closer to the present, conditions had changed. Thus, the larger islands have much more pristine volcanic features due to their more recent formation and lesser amounts of rainfall. Again, the Bible's record of the past is an important starting point in developing models to correctly understand how the Galápagos were formed, how the soils on the islands formed, and how past processes differ from present-day processes.

JOHN WHITMORE

Pāhoehoe lava

THE VOLCANOES OF the Galápagos Islands have varied shapes, eruptive histories, and compositions. The seven volcanoes of Isabela and Fernandina islands are large shield volcanoes with well-developed craters, but they differ conspicuously from the familiar shield volcanoes of Hawaii. Whereas the Hawaiian volcanoes are very broad with gently sloping sides, the Galápagos volcanoes have slopes that steepen abruptly, giving them a distinctive "inverted soup-bowl" outline.

Eruptions have occurred either from fissures around the craters or from vents and fissures lower on the sides. Where side-branching fissures have developed laterally from these volcanoes and lava flows from them, parasitic cones developed. If gas bubbles were in those lavas, they erupted explosively, sending showers of ash up into the air that fell back and landed around the vents, forming cinder cones.

The volcanoes on the other islands are very different from the volcanoes of Fernandina and Isabela. Floreana is a roughly circular, low shield whose outline is dominated by numerous cinder cones. Santiago is an elongated shield. Rábida consists mainly of a cluster of steep-sided domes, with the remains of two cinder cones at its northern base. Pinzón is a small shield volcano with two overlapping craters. Santa Cruz is a gently sloping, elliptical shield. San Cristóbal has the longest history of activity, having had at least five recognizable episodes of eruptions. An older shield volcano dominates its southwestern half, while the northeastern half consists primarily of relatively young lava flows erupted from fissures.

Santa Fé and Española are the only two major Galápagos islands that are different. Once thought to be uplifted large areas of seafloor, subsequent investigations have determined that both islands consist primarily of lava erupted on land, rather than underwater. Though a number of small cinder cones have been identified on each island, various indicators suggest that the main vents for Santa Fé and Española lie offshore. The islands are probably remnants of somewhat larger shield volcanoes.

The volcanic rocks on all the Galápagos Islands are dark (usually black) and very fine-grained basalts, similar to those found on the Hawaiian Islands. And similar to the Hawaiian volcanoes, the Galápagos Island volcanoes have erupted quietly (non-explosively) and the lava flows cooled as pahoehoe and aa types, the former having smooth, ropy, or billowy surfaces, and the latter rough, jagged surfaces. Even though mass destruction is usually associated with volcanoes, there is beauty in their varied shapes and picturesque patterns of the lava fields.

ANDREW SNELLING

19

Volcano Cerro Azul

Parasitic cones on Bartolomé

Aa lava on Isabela

HOW OLD ARE the Galápagos Islands? The volcanic lava flows throughout the islands have been subjected to potassium-argon (K-Ar) and argon-argon (^{40}Ar-^{39}Ar) radiometric dating. The oldest lava flows dated by those methods occur on Española (3.04 and 3.31 million years old). In contrast, lava flows on Isabela date to much less than a million years.

But how reliable are these dates? All the dated lava flows erupted only recently since the Flood, so they can't be millions of years old. However, we need to remember that these radiometric methods depend on three crucial assumptions.

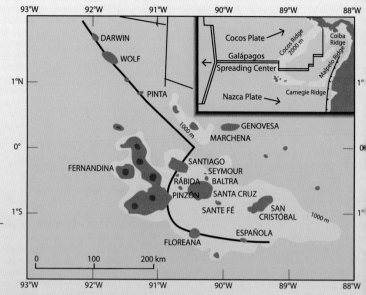

Map of the Galápagos Archipelago. The bold line shows the inferred fault system that seperates thin, weak oceanic crust to the north and east from stronger and thicker oceanic crust to the south and west. The inset shows the regional tectonic setting, with the Galápagos Archipelago at the western end of the Carnegie Ridge. Courtesy of Dr. Andrew Snelling and the Institute for Creation Research.

Conditions at Time Zero	Can we be sure all the argon (daughter material) in these lavas was produced by radioactive decay of potassium (parent material)? Many recently erupted lava flows are known to contain argon that was added to them from the volcanic gases, making young rocks appear millions of years old. (The more argon that is present, the older the rock is assumed to be.)
No Contamination	Can we be sure there was no contamination or weathering of the lavas that added or removed potassium respectively? As the molten rock rises from the volcano, potassium can be added to the lava. (Addition of potassium would make the rock appear younger, and removal of potassium would make the rock appear older.)
Constant Decay Rate	Has the potassium always decayed at today's slow measured rate? There are several lines of evidence that support the idea that radioactive decay rates were much faster in the recent past. With such unreliable "clocks" ticking at faster unknown rates in the past, they simply cannot be used to "tell the time"!

None of these assumptions are provable, because geologists were not present when these lavas erupted to observe whether there was no addition of argon,

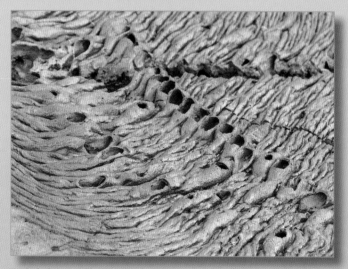

Exploded gas bubbles in pahoehoe lava

contamination, or weathering, and how fast potassium was decaying. In fact, when they have been present for the eruption of lavas, those lavas have sometimes yielded totally wrong grossly old ages. These assumptions are not reasonable, and radiometric dating methods cannot yield the absolute ages claimed for these lavas.

If the K-Ar ages of the lavas are plotted against their distance from Fernandina (the youngest island), then the ages of the oldest flows on each of the islands form a reasonable progression from youngest in the west on Fernandina to oldest in the east on Española and San Cristóbal. This is consistent with the movement of the Nazca Plate over the Galápagos hot spot as the islands formed.

So what is the true age of the Galápagos Islands? The first volcanoes began erupting as the Flood ended, and soon after the islands progressively formed in the few hundred years that followed, with occasional eruptions continuing to the present. Since the Flood ended about 4,350 years ago, the Galápagos Islands are less than 4,350 years old.

ANDREW SNELLING

Who made heaven and earth, the sea, and all
that is in them; Who keeps truth forever,
                              —Psalm 146:6

WITH ITS DARK skies and its position astraddle the earth's equator, the Galápagos Islands are a wonderful place to enjoy the night sky. Most striking are the stars that we can't see from most of the Northern Hemisphere, such as the Southern Cross. Along with its distinctive shape, the Southern Cross contains several fainter star clusters that are best viewed with binoculars. The Jewel Box cluster with its colorful stars is a particularly stunning part of this constellation. Most breathtaking and a short distance from the Milky Way's center are the Large Magellanic Cloud (LMC) and the Small Magellanic Cloud (SMC). When compared to our own, these small satellite galaxies look as if they have been cast out from the Milky Way. Both contain millions of stars and they are a delight to scan with binoculars.

The four bright stars that form the Southern Cross are within 400 light years of earth. Many of the stars, clusters, and nebulae along the Milky Way are thousands of light years away, but the Magellanic Clouds are farther still. The LMC is about 160,000 light years away, while the SMC is 200,000 light years. But if the earth is only several thousand years old as the Bible suggests, how can the LMC and SMC be seen, since they are much farther than 6,000 light years away? This is a very good question, and biblical creationists have even called this the light-travel time problem. There are several proposed solutions to this problem.

One answer is that God created the universe mature, much as He did Adam and Eve, so that light arrived here from the beginning so that stars could fulfill their functions (Genesis 1:14–18). However, this explanation has some problems and several creation physicists and astronomers have developed ideas based upon Einstein's theory of general relativity. General relativity is a well-tested theory of how space and time work. These newer explanations use the principle of time dilation to explain how light arrived on the earth very quickly. The important thing to realize is that God created this marvelous earth, the entire universe, and everything in it in six days. Once we realize that He is powerful enough to create everything, we understand that it was a simple matter to get the light from the stars to earth within the biblical time frame.

DANNY FAULKNER

Small and Large Magellanic Clouds

THE EQUATORIAL LOCATION of the Galápagos Islands allows visitors to see both northern and southern sky objects. Stars rise straight up from the eastern horizon, arcing up and then set straight down on the western horizon. Only from earth's equator are all the stars in God's heavens (viewable from earth) visible at one time or another during the year. Among the most amazing starry assemblages in the heavens are globular clusters (GCs). GCs are round-shaped, rich clusters of stars (usually 50,000–10,000,000) that travel around their galaxies at random tilts and elliptical orbits, much like comets in orbit about the solar system. Their combined orbits create the halo that encircles the galaxies. Toward the north sits a wonderful GC, M13, in the keystone of the constellation Hercules. But in the south, globular clusters are magnificent! Omega Centauri appears about the size of the full moon to the unaided eye. Appearing nearly twice as large as the moon is another GC, 47 Tuc. It is easily visible to the eye, and is a glorious sight in binoculars (near the Small Magellanic Cloud).

Omega Centauri

GCs are a part of what astronomers call population II (pop II) objects. Pop II are high velocity objects with negligible interstellar dust or gas. However, globular clusters should gradually accumulate dust or gas from steady stellar winds and outflows from their stars. If GCs are billions of years old, why don't we see this dust and gas? Astronomers have hypothesized mechanisms to remove, or clear, the dust and gas from the clusters. The most robust mechanism for clearing the dust and gas from GCs happens only every 100 million to one billion years. Given the secular time frame of a 13.82-billion-year-old universe, the GCs should contain 10 to 100 times more dust and gas than we actually observe (based on the relatively slow clearing process). The only conclusion is that these objects are young — much younger than the 12-billion-year-old age for GCs accepted by the secular astronomical community and more in line with the age of the universe proposed by the biblical creation community. Again, the heavens support the biblical worldview founded in the Book of Genesis!

RON SAMEC

23

The unique flora and fauna of the Galápagos Islands stem from an unusual convergence of ocean currents near the islands. As the world "settled down" after Noah's Flood, the Galápagos Islands rose slowly from the sea, the result of multiple volcanic eruptions. Ocean currents also began to form, and three currents converged at different times of the year near the Galápagos. The existence of currents like these was noted by David in Psalm 8:8 when he wrote that fish "pass through the paths of the seas."

Matthew Fontaine Maury was a U.S. naval navigator who was well versed in the Psalms from his early childhood. He sought to understand and chart these "paths of the seas" to make ship navigation easier, efficient, and less dangerous. He was so successful that he is credited with being the father of modern oceanography. Maury believed God's Word was trustworthy and held it as the utmost authority in all his scientific endeavors. In a university speech he stated,

I have been blamed by men of science, both in this country and in England, for quoting the Bible in confirmation of the doctrines of physical geography. The Bible, they say, was not written for scientific purposes, and is therefore of no authority in matters of science. I beg pardon! The Bible is authority for everything it touches. . . . The Bible is true and science is true, and therefore each, if truly read, but proves the truth of the other.

When I, a pioneer in one department of this beautiful science, discover the truths of Revelation and the truths of science reflecting light the one upon the other, how can I, as a truth-loving, knowledge-seeking man, fail to point out the beauty and rejoice in its discovery?[1]

The Bible is not a science textbook, which is good because they change all the time! However, God is unchanging and cannot lie (Malachi 3:6; Titus 1:2), so His Word can be trusted. Creation scientists begin with the truth of God's Word as the foundation to build models about what happened in the past (historical science). These scientists have

24

discovered, just as Matthew Maury did, that what we observe in the world (observational science) confirms the truth of the science and history in God's Word.

The convergence of ocean currents near Galápagos greatly affects its climate. The islands are not the lush tropical rainforests that people expect to find at equatorial destinations. Instead the climate varies from humid (tropical) in the higher elevations to arid (desert) in the lower elevations, with many of these zones appearing on the same islands. The islands have two major seasons — wet and dry. During the wet season the islands are very colorful, with green leaves, yellow cactus flowers, and pink morning glories. But in the few weeks following the end of the wet season, most plants turn brown. As a result, many of the animals that have colonized the islands became dependent on the ocean for food.

How did animals get to the Galápagos Islands? After the Flood, God commanded the animals to "multiply and fill the earth" (Genesis 8:17). The animals may have traveled to various parts of the world by rafting on vegetation debris, flying, drifting on ocean currents, or being carried by humans. God designed animals to fill all parts of the earth and those arriving at the Galápagos began to inhabit both the land and the sea.

Those inhabiting the sea can be greatly affected by weather extremes such as El Niño. Many people are familiar with weather changes that occur every few years in relation to El Niño, but nowhere are these changes more vividly seen than in the Galápagos. In El Niño years, air and water temperatures increase along with a dramatic increase in precipitation. During the 1982–83 El Niño, 127 inches of

Galápagos penguin

rain fell on the island of Santa Cruz (normal rainfall is 8 inches per year)! Temperature and precipitation changes greatly affect the plants and animals on the islands.

During El Niño years, sea lions, penguins, and marine iguanas greatly decrease in number. In the 1982–83 El Niño event, the population of Galápagos penguins declined by 77 percent and marine iguana populations have been seen to decrease by 90 percent during El Niño years. Scientists are concerned because large population crashes decrease the genetic diversity of the remaining populations, potentially making them more susceptible to disease. Efforts are underway to study and protect many of these species since they are unique to the Galápagos.

---

1   Quote from Matthew Fontaine Maury address to the University of the South (Tennessee) in 1860, Diana (Nannie) Fontaine Corbin, *A Life of Matthew Fontaine Maury* (London: S. Low, Marston, Searle, & Rivington, 1888), p. 178.

And God made the beast of the earth according to its kind, cattle according to its kind, and everything that creeps on the earth according to its kind. And God saw that it was good.

—Genesis 1:25

Although El Niño events have been occurring for several thousand years, animal populations still thrive in the Galápagos. God foreknew that the Fall and Flood would occur and designed animals to change and survive in a sin-cursed world. Marine iguanas have the ability to decrease their body size during El Niño events so they require less food. Darwin's finches appear to have the ability to sense El Niño events before they arrive. They will mate differently, forming hybrid offspring (a combination of two different finch species) that are more vigorous.

If God cares this much for finches, how much more does He care for us (Matthew 10:29–31)! I hope you will see the many ways that weather and currents affect the Galápagos Islands and how the Creator has shown His care for creation as you hear from those who have studied this exotic location.

Marine iguana

Galápagos finch

WHEN THE GALÁPAGOS Islands rose from the sea after the Flood, they were probably greeted by a rather confused pattern of wind and waves. For many years the oceans were likely much warmer and more uniform in temperature from the equator to the poles. Since the temperature difference between the poles and the equator drives the atmospheric circulation, it's likely that large-scale weather patterns and ocean circulations were much weaker for a few hundred years.

As the Andes Mountains in South America quickly rose during and following the Flood, they likely established a local weather pattern due to temperature differences between land, sea, and mountains. There was probably less difference in the weather between summer and winter. The proximity of the cold Andes next to the warm Pacific Ocean resulted in the rapid development of glaciers on the mountains and downslope winds

28

As water wears away stones, and as torrents wash away the soil of the earth; …

—Job 14:19

along the entire west coast of South America. As the oceans cooled, the increasing temperature difference in the ocean and atmosphere between the poles and the equator began to form global circulations. A clockwise gyre (rotating current) of wind and water began to form in the North Pacific and a counter-clockwise gyre in the South Pacific. Jet streams began to develop in the Northern and Southern Hemispheres along with stormy conditions.

Today, the North Pacific and South Pacific gyres flow westward across the Pacific Ocean on the north and south sides of the equator. But directly over the equator, a counter-current of water flows eastward until it hits Ecuador. Near the Galápagos Islands the currents are highly complex. The northward-flowing Humboldt Current, the southward-flowing Panama Current, and the equatorial counter-current alternately bathe the islands in cold, nutrient-rich water and warm, nutrient-poor water. An annual oscillation of cold and warm water causes cool, dry conditions from June through December and warm, rainy conditions from January to May.

In addition to this normal annual cycle, a three– to seven–year oscillation of warm sea-surface water crosses the Pacific Ocean from west to east and produces alternating droughts and floods over a multi-year period. This poorly understood El Niño/Southern Oscillation starts with warming sea-surface temperatures and rising surface pressure over the Indian Ocean, Indonesia, and Australia. The warm region moves slowly eastward to South America. Trade winds and rainfall over the Southern Pacific are affected, eventually resulting in rain in the normally dry eastern Pacific, the Galápagos, and the deserts of Peru. A major die-off of plants and animals in the Galápagos Islands occurs during the drought years and luxurious growth in the wet years. These cycles are important causes of the amazing diversity and survivability of plants and animals found in the islands. The Bible is an important starting point in developing models to correctly understand past ocean and weather patterns in relation to the Flood and how they differ from those in the present.

LARRY VARDIMAN

Let the rivers clap their hands;
Let the hills be joyful together before the Lord

—Psalm 98:8

30

FOR AN EQUATORIAL location, the Galápagos Islands have a complex climate. The islands lie at the boundaries of three major ocean currents that determine the climate. Two are surface currents and one is a current below the surface layer. The cold, nutrient-rich Humboldt Current flows north from Antarctica along the South American coast to near the equator. The Panama Current spreads warm, nutrient-poor water southward from the Northern Hemisphere to the equator, where convergence with the Humboldt Current causes both currents to be diverted west toward the Galápagos Islands. The third current is the Cromwell Current below the surface layer that flows toward the east along the equator, forcing the water upward upon meeting the islands and bringing cool, nutrient-rich water to the surface.

The surface currents, determined by the average wind speed, shift with the season. The southeast trade winds blowing from about June to December push the Humboldt Current into the Galápagos Islands, resulting in a cooler, cloudier dry season at coastal locations. Maximum temperatures are generally in the mid- to upper-70s. Because of the mountainous terrain, the southeast trade winds force air upward, where it condenses to form clouds. The light rain from these clouds falls in the highlands, producing lush vegetation on the larger islands.

The southeast trade winds weaken during December and January, and the northeast trade winds pick up, spreading the warmer water of the Panama Current into the Galápagos Islands. This causes the wet season from January to May with warmer daytime temperatures in the mid-80s and abundant precipitation. There is actually more sun and blue skies during the wet season, but the warmer sea surface and air temperatures cause showers and thundershowers to develop rapidly.

The animals on the islands are generally adapted to the wet and dry seasons at low altitude. However, a major cyclical climate change called El Niño causes a much different climate on the islands and wreaks havoc on the animal populations. Because the warm water during El Niño is nutrient poor, there is a mass die-off of marine micro-organisms, which spreads up the food chain, causing the death of fish, which in turn causes the death of sea birds, sea lions, and marine iguanas. But some animals, such as flamingos, flourish because warmer lagoon water increases the shrimp population that the flamingos eat. Even amid such extreme changes in weather on a yearly basis and during El Niño events, there is beauty seen in the landscape and the diversity of plants and animals that have been designed by God to adapt and survive in this harsh environment.

MIKE OARD

31

Swallowtail gull

THE GALÁPAGOS ISLANDS are exceptional in that they are positioned at the confluence (meeting) of major ocean currents. These currents are critical to ocean life and weather patterns. Specifically, the surface currents driven mainly by the winds affect the climate of the Galápagos Islands.

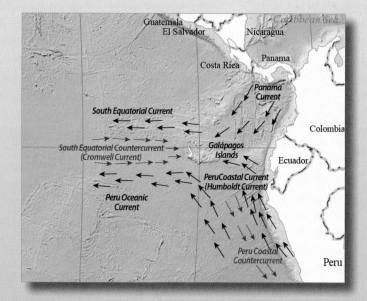

The phenomenon of oceanic nutrient upwelling contributes to the fauna and flora of the Galápagos Islands. Upwelling occurs in the oceans when wind-driven motion of cooler, dense, nutrient-rich water rises to the ocean surface and the warmer surface waters are replaced. Zones caused by winds blowing parallel to shore may cause upwelling and are identified by elevated phytoplankton (microscopic organisms that photosynthesize) and cool sea-surface temperatures. Upwelling also occurs in northward-moving Antarctic waters that stimulate production of primary producers such as phytoplankton. Zooplankton (microscopic organisms that do not photosynthesize) consume this phytoplankton that in turn contributes to abundant marine life within the Galápagos archipelago.

Cromwell Current

This current flows eastward, originating from the deeper areas of the western Pacific Ocean. This very cold flow runs as a subsurface or undercurrent (running about 300 feet beneath surface currents) carrying a volume equivalent to half the Gulf Stream. The Cromwell Current extends the length of the equator, is 250 miles wide, and heads straight into the Galápagos Islands. It is rich in both nutrients and oxygen, supporting a wide selection of marine animals. Indeed, much of the nutrient-rich upwelled water comes from this equatorial undercurrent.

Humboldt Current

This current is a significant contributor of the upwelling and a dominant contributor to the climate of the Galápagos Islands during the summer and fall. The Humboldt is a cold, low-salinity current that moves up from Antarctica and continues along the west coast of South America. It runs from June to December. The Humboldt Current cools the islands, producing a subtropical climate, and combined with southeast winds, produces an inversion layer. The result is a low cloud covering the islands during the day. One result of this weather pattern is a light mist forming in the highlands and moving to the shore that the locals call garúa season. Visibility in the waters surrounding the islands is lowered due to blooms of plankton. This increases food availability and marine animal activity.

Panama Current

As the Humboldt Current begins to ebb in December, the Panama Current replaces it and is active from January to May. Not surprisingly, the warmer water (70° to 80°F) this current affects the climate of the islands, reducing the inversion layer that is present from June to December and clears the skies and waters allowing easy viewing of the many marine species.

The confluence of these currents and the resulting weather patterns lead to diverse ecosystems on the islands inhabited by plants and animals found nowhere else in the world.

FRANK SHERWIN

33

THE GALÁPAGOS ISLANDS are home to a wide range of diverse ecosystems. The diversity is due to a phenomenon known as the rain shadow effect. Winds blowing across the ocean carry water vapor, and when they strike high elevation islands they are directed upward. Water vapor condenses into liquid droplets as they meet cooler air, and rain or mist (garúa) is produced in the higher elevations making them humid. Lower elevations are arid. This phenomenon results in seven distinct ecological zones (or ecosystems) on the islands, each with differing plant and animal life. The bigger islands with higher elevations have the most zones.

Let us take an imaginary journey from the highest elevations on one of the big islands, like Santa Cruz, and hike toward the sea. Though we may walk a mere six miles, it will feel like we have experienced seven completely different worlds along the way.

Pampa Zone

Miconia Zone

At 3,000 feet or higher, we find a wet and misty place with no trees or shrubs. Only found on older islands with high elevations, this is the coolest and wettest of zones averaging 5 feet of rain annually with some years experiencing 16 feet. Soil accumulates and fills cracks between rocks that allows for standing water resulting in swamps and bogs consisting of mosses, ferns, and sedges. One amazing exception to these low-growing plants is the beautiful tree fern that is periodically scattered throughout this zone and can be 30 feet tall.

At 1,950–2,300 feet, we are finding it difficult to maneuver through the dense shrubs. Looking closer at these shrubs, you will notice the purple flowers and beautiful yellow and red leaf edges. These are the Galápagos *Miconia*, and this zone is named for them.

Brown Zone

This zone is transitional between the Miconia and Scalesia zones. It is dominated by a tree known as Cat's Claw that has long thorns and can grow into nearly impenetrable walls of vegetation. On some islands, we'd be lucky to get through it without torn clothes. These trees, in turn, are covered with other organisms such as mosses, ferns, and lichens. Because they grow on Cat's Claw bark and do not take nutrients from the tree, they are called epiphytes. Together, they are important in capturing water and allowing it to drip into pools that are important bathing and drinking areas for Galápagos tortoises.

Scalesia Zone

From June to December the ghostly garúa mists that surround us allow only for sighting silhouettes of the trees that make up this dense forest. We are roughly 970–1,970 feet above sea level and in the lowest of the humid zones. The silhouetted trees are *Scalesia pedunculata*, part of the sunflower family, which produce white daisy-like flowers. Water in the soil is not retained well but plants obtain sufficient water from the garúa. Here we will also find the dome-backed Galápagos tortoises.

Transition Zone

At 300 to 700 feet, we arrive in the boundary zone that transitions us from humid environments to arid ones. For the lower elevation islands this may mark the uppermost ecological zone, and for this reason they are called desert islands. Pega-pega ("stick-stick") is a common tree here. It gets its name from the numerous lichens that grow on the tree making it "sticky." From here down, keep your eyes open because there is a good chance of sighting the saddleback tortoises.

Arid Zone

Reaching 300 feet and moving toward the sea, you'll notice it is dry and hot. The dominant plant life includes three types of cacti: candelabra, lava, and prickly pear. Palo Santo is another common tree we see, with white bark that only produces leaves in the dry season.

Coastal/ Littoral Zone

The hardened lava fields we have walked on to reach water's edge are even more common on the younger islands. Vegetation in these lagoons are salt tolerant, like mangroves, and we also see crabs and marine iguanas.

The variety of life found throughout these ecosystems is a wonderful reminder of the creativity of the Creator.

TOM HENNIGAN

Pioneer plants mollugo and tiquilia on lava fields

37

THE BIBLE DOESN'T give us all the historical details; often just "broad brush stokes." Because humans are curious creatures, this generates questions. One major question that pops to mind is how the various animals got to where they currently are from Noah's ark. The problem arises when we consider island animals, hundreds to thousands of miles away from the nearest continent, which don't seem capable of crossing that much ocean without the help of man.

The whole context of the Flood is an account of God using natural means to bring salvation to Noah's family and the animals of the ark. God used physical means to accomplish both salvation and judgment. He had Noah build a very big ark, involving a lot of hard work and time. God could have supernaturally saved Noah, his family, and the animals by teleporting them off the planet for a year while He flooded the earth. But He didn't. He had a physical man build a physical ark to save physical people and animals from physical drowning. That is why it is in keeping with the way God accomplished His ultimate purpose to explain the current location of animals using natural movements that we can comprehend.

Galápagos birds and insects are easy to explain; they simply flew. Even non-migratory birds like Darwin's finches, and insects that are poorly adapted to flying great distances, could have been picked up and transported there by great oceanic storms. Even the flightless Galápagos cormorant probably descended from flying ancestors. After many generations of flight being unnecessary, or even a liability for survival, they lost the ability to fly.

Because reptiles are ectothermic (cold-blooded) and don't have to burn a lot of food to maintain a high body temperature, they can go

Swallowtail gull

Flightless cormorant

for very long periods of time without food. When torrential rainfall on the mainland causes rivers to overflow, often trees and large amounts of vegetation are ripped off the riverbanks and carried out to sea as great floating rafts with various animals still clinging to them. These can drift for hundreds to thousands of miles carrying hapless reptilian refugees with them. If these rafts wash up on the shore of an island, the passengers can clamber off and successfully colonize the island.

This could have been the case with the Galápagos land iguanas, lava lizards, and tortoises. Tortoises are buoyant and could drift on the currents. All of these reptiles could have descended from closely related species that lived on the mainland of South America or even Africa. God created the various kinds with great genetic capacity to adapt to an array of habitats. The differences the Galápagos species exhibit in size and shape from their mainland ancestors could arise

after many generations of natural selection (and other mechanisms) that successfully bring out those divinely designed traits best suited to their new home. Because mammals are much more sensitive to heat loss and starvation, it is unlikely for them to survive this type of slow, rafting journey. This is why islands farthest away from continents often do not have indigenous (native) mammals.

We also must not rule out the possibility of Galápagos resident animals getting there by boat after the confusion of languages at Babel (Genesis 11). Phoenicians were skilled mariners plying the oceans many hundreds of years before Christ. As we know, live animals were brought on board for food. It is likely that Phoenicians sailed around the southern tip of Africa. If they could do that, they could have gone much farther than we know; even around Cape Horn of South America. Recent genetic analysis indicates that the

Yellow-crowned night heron

Land iguana

Galápagos tortoises are more closely related to African hinge-back tortoises. This finding suggests that the most recent mainland ancestor of the Galápagos tortoises may have hailed from Africa, not South America.

The Phoenicians (or some other ancient mariners) may have brought the first tortoises. They are low-maintenance food aboard ships because they can live long periods without food or water. In fact, the Galápagos tortoises were often used this way in the 19th century by whaling ships. Regardless of how the animals arrived in the Galápagos, they came a long way in fulfilling God's command to "multiply on the earth" (Genesis 8:17).

GORDON WILSON

Galápagos tortoise

Marine iguana

THE AMAZING GROUP of animals in the Galápagos Islands share these miraculous experiences with all air-breathing, land-dwelling animals in the world: 1) They were created by the Lord Jesus Christ at the end of creation week; 2) they were "subjected to futility" (Romans 8:20) when Adam and Eve sinned; and 3) they were preserved in the ark for over a year during the global Flood.

These animals entered the ark, and 371 days later came out of the ark. Then began God's providential work of animal migration around this entire planet! All the animals fulfilled God's command to "be fruitful and multiply on the earth" (Genesis 8:17). Some of the animals eventually went as far as the newly formed Galápagos Islands off the coast of South America.

Thank You, Lord, for telling us something of Your special care for animals! And infinitely more of Your gracious provision for human beings who were created in Your image and likeness and whose sins were paid for on the Cross of Calvary! May every animal, bird, and reptile around the world remind us of "how great Thou art!"

JOHN C. WHITCOMB

One of the central reasons that the Galápagos Islands are well known today is because of a visit in 1835 by Charles Darwin, the father of biological evolution. While his visit to the Galápagos played a role in his development of evolutionary ideas, many other factors also contributed to his ideas. Darwin was raised in a minimally religious home. Although he studied medicine and prepared for the priesthood, he eventually became a naturalist. Darwin's theological views were greatly impacted by mentors and others throughout his education. These individuals wanted to radically change society because of their belief that God did not exist.

In 1831, Darwin was asked to be a naturalist on the *Beagle*, a ship that would survey and chart coasts all over the world. By this time, Darwin was already convinced that the history presented in the Old Testament was false and thus, the 6,000-year age of the earth inferred from Scripture could not be correct. On the ship Darwin brought with him Charles Lyell's *Principles of Geology*. Lyell popularized the idea of uniformitarianism, that present-day geological processes were the same processes that shaped the earth in the past. He dismissed the biblical history of Noah's catastrophic Flood and was convinced that millions of years of slow processes had formed the earth. Dismissal of the Bible's history and the endorsement of millions of years of time provided an important foundation for Darwin's development of evolutionary ideas.

Many people think Darwin developed the idea of molecules-to-man evolution as a direct result of visiting the Galápagos Islands and studying the finches that later bore his name. Although this is incorrect, his trip to the islands and study of the animals there were very influential to his thinking about evolution. Reflecting on his visit to the islands, Darwin wrote,

When I recollect the fact that [from] the form of the body, shape of the scales and general size, the Spaniards can at once pronounce from which island any tortoise may have been brought; when I see these islands in sight of each other and possessed of but a scanty stock of animals, tenanted by these birds, but slightly differing in structures and filling the same place in nature; I must suspect they are only varieties. [1]

Darwin is referring to the observation that specific "varieties" or species of tortoises, mockingbirds, etc. are associated with specific islands. This is an example of good observational science. Darwin concluded that the tortoises on the different islands were all part of the tortoise family with variation in traits, like shell shape, among the different islands. At this point he was merely proposing variation within an animal kind, not one kind of animal evolving into a different kind of animal (or molecules-to-man evolution).

However, Darwin then ventured into the realm of historical science when he wrote,

Let a pair be introduced [to an area] and increase slowly, from many enemies, so as often to intermarry; who will dare say what the result. According to this view, animals on separate islands, ought to become different if kept long enough apart, with slightly differ[ent] circumstances. [2]

And as his biographers note, "thirty pages later in the notebook, he drew his historic branching diagram showing how different species might be linked to each other by common descent."[3] Darwin had dismissed the biblical time frame of 6,000 years for the age of the earth and now had millions of years (provided through Lyell's ideas) over which changes in animals could occur. The evolutionary model that he developed (historical science) was based on the belief that man's ideas about the past are correct and not God's Word. He believed the small differences he observed that led to variation within a kind (observational science) could eventually lead to large changes that would allow one kind of animal to evolve into a completely different kind of animal over millions of years (historical science). To put it simply, Darwin started with a false authority for his beliefs about the past, and that false assumption led him to develop false ideas about how animals change over time.

Darwin's beliefs about the existence of God and the truth of His Word were also impacted by his observation that nature was cruel and destructive. Darwin wrote,

I cannot persuade myself that a beneficent and omnipotent God would have designedly created the Ichneumonidae [wasp]

1   Charles Darwin, quoted in Nora Barlow, editor, "Darwin's Ornithological Notes," *Bulletin of the British Museum (Natural History), Historical Series 2*, no. 7: 262. Online at http://darwin-online.org.uk/content/frameset?viewtype=text&itemID=F1577&pageseq=1.

2   Charles Darwin, "Notebook B: [Transmutation of Species (1837–1838)]," transcribed by Kees Rookmaaker, Darwin Online, http://darwin-online.org.uk/content/frameset?itemID=CUL-DAR121.-&viewtype=text&pageseq=1.

3   Gordon Chancellor and Randal Keynes, "Darwin's Field Notes on the Galápagos: 'A Little World within Itself,'" Darwin Online, http://darwin-online.org.uk/EditorialIntroductions/Chancellor_Keynes_Galapagos.html.

with the express intention of their feeding within the living bodies of Caterpillars, or that a cat should play with mice.[4]

Darwin could not understand how there could be a loving God and death and suffering in the world at the same time. By not starting with the foundation of God's Word, Darwin failed to understand that death and suffering in the world are man's fault, not God's. Adam and Eve chose to sin (disobey God) and as a result there is death and suffering in this world (Genesis 3). Although evolutionists may see death as a hero in the upward progress of living creatures, they know in their heart of hearts (Romans 1:18) that death is instead a destructive intruder (Romans 8:22).

But are Darwin's evolutionary ideas his real legacy? Sadly, no. Darwin's evolutionary ideas eliminated the need for a God who is intimately involved with His creation because he proposed that all living things came to exist in their present form by natural processes. If humans are nothing more than animals, then morality is irrelevant. Just as we don't charge a cat with first-degree murder for killing a mouse, why should we say killing human babies in the womb is wrong? The moral relativism that pervades our culture today is, in part, founded upon the lie that the creature is the creator (evolution over millions of years) and not the eternal God

(Romans 1:23–25). If a law-giving God does not exist, then there is no basis for right and wrong and man can do what is "right in his own eyes" (Judges 21:25).

Darwin's real legacy also impacts the gospel. If evolution is true, then the gospel is robbed of its power. According to Scripture, only mankind was created in the image of God (Genesis 1:26–27), and because of that, we can have a relationship with God. That relationship was broken in the Garden of Eden when Adam and Eve sinned (Genesis 3) and restoration was made possible by the death and Resurrection of the Last Adam, Jesus Christ, who as both God and sinless man (Hebrews 4:15) perfectly bore the image of God (Hebrews 1:3). Because of Adam's sin, all mankind sins and dies (Romans 5:12), but because of God's grace through Jesus's death on the Cross, eternal life is promised to all who believe (Romans 5:21). If humans are not unique, special creations of God created to bear His image but are simply evolved animals, then Jesus's death on the Cross is meaningless. The history in Genesis is foundational knowledge to the true power of the gospel that Jesus Christ died for sinful man (Romans 5:8), not animals.

Charles Darwin left a legacy that was bigger than himself and that has impacted millions of people — for the worse. How have you been impacted by his legacy?

---

4   Francis Darwin, editor, *The Life and Letters of Charles Darwin*, Vol. II (New York: Appleton, 1987), p. 105.

"*Look at the birds of the air, for they neither sow nor reap nor gather into barns; yet your heavenly Father feeds them. Are you not of more value than they?*

—Matthew 6:26

45

Blue-footed boobies
dive-bombing for food

CHARLES DARWIN IS well known for his biological theory of evolution by natural selection but it is important to understand the theological and geological influences that provided the foundation for his ideas. Though Charles never knew his paternal grandfather, Erasmus Darwin, Erasmus' theologically liberal and evolutionary ideas expressed in his two-volume *Zoönomia* (1794–96) significantly influenced him, so much so that Charles used the same title for his notebook of ideas about evolution that he started writing in 1837.[5] Charles' father, Robert, was even more of an unbeliever, bordering on atheism,[6] and his mother was a Unitarian.[7]

Robert Edmond Grant mentored Darwin while he was a medical student at Edinburgh University (1825–27). Grant was a rabid atheistic evolutionist "committed to a radical overhaul of science and society."[8] He was also much influenced by similar evolutionist and social radicals, some of a Unitarian bent, in the Plinian Society founded by the old-earth Professor of Natural History, Robert Jameson.[9]

But in the end Darwin couldn't stomach medicine, so his father insisted that he attend Cambridge in 1828 to prepare for the Anglican priesthood, which would provide Darwin with a nice living. Darwin tells us,

> I liked the thought of being a country clergyman . . . and as I did not then in the least doubt the strict and literal truth of every

5   Adrian Desmond and James Moore, *Darwin* (London: Michael Joseph, 1991), p. 229.

6   Ian Taylor, *In the Minds of Men: Darwin and the New World Order* (Foley, MN: TFE Publishing, 2008), p. 113–114.

7   Desmond and Moore, *Darwin*, p. 12–13.

8   Ibid, p. 34. Desmond and Moore describe Grant's influence as Darwin "coming under the wing of an uncompromising evolutionist." In Darwin's autobiography, he says that he didn't embrace Grant's and his grandfather's evolutionary ideas at the time, but then added, "Nevertheless it is probable that the hearing rather early in life such views maintained and praised may have favoured my upholding them under a different form in my *Origin of Species*." See Nora Barlow, editor, *The Autobiography of Charles Darwin, 1809–1882* (New York: W.W. Norton, 1958), p. 49.

9   Desmond and Moore, *Darwin*, p. 31–32.

He shall be like a tree planted by the rivers of water, that brings forth its fruit in its season, whose leaf also shall not wither; and whatever he does shall prosper.

—Psalm 1:3

Black Turtle Cove is a mangrove estuary on the northern shores of Santa Cruz Island. Many rays, sea turtles, pelicans, and other wildlife live among the mangroves.

word of the Bible, I soon persuaded myself that our Creed must be fully accepted. It never struck me how illogical it was to say that I believed in what I could not understand and what is in fact unintelligible.[10]

Despite his claim to believe the Bible, from his family background and upbringing it is safe to say that he was certainly no orthodox Christian. His remarks about his thinking just a few years later confirm this conclusion:

> Whilst on board the *Beagle* I was quite orthodox, and I remember being heartily laughed at by several of the officers (though themselves orthodox) for quoting the Bible as an unanswerable authority on some point of morality. I suppose it was the novelty of the argument that amused them. But I had gradually come, by this time, to see that the Old Testament from its manifestly false history of the world, with the Tower of Babel, the rainbow as a sign, etc., etc., and from its attributing to God the feelings of a revengeful tyrant, was no more to be trusted than the sacred books of the Hindus, or the beliefs of the barbarian.[11]

Of course Darwin's theological views greatly affected his scientific views especially as it pertained to the past. Most important to Darwin's geological thinking was Charles Lyell, who as a deist (or Unitarian) [12] sought to "free the science of geology from Moses."[13] Darwin informs us that on the Beagle:

---

10 Barlow, *Autobiography of Charles Darwin*, p. 56–57.

11 Barlow, *Autobiography of Charles Darwin*, p. 85.

12 John Hedley Brooke, *Science and Religion: Some Historical Perspectives* (Cambridge, UK: Cambridge Univ. Press, 1991), p. 251.

13 Charles Lyell, quoted in Katherine Lyell, *Life, Letters and Journals of Sir Charles Lyell, Bart.,* Vol. 1 (London: John Murray, 1881), p. 268.

I had brought with me the first volume of Lyell's *Principles of Geology,* which I studied attentively; and this book was of the highest service to me in many ways.[14]

Darwin later commented,

He who can read Sir Charles Lyell's grand work on the *Principles of Geology,* which the future historian will recognize as having produced a revolution in natural science, yet does not admit how incomprehensibly vast have been the past periods of time, may at once close this volume.[15]

We can also see this influence of Lyell in Darwin's famous journal entry during his study of the Santa Cruz river valley in Argentina, just a few stops before he reached the Galápagos Islands. He wrote:

The river, though it has so little power in transporting even inconsiderable fragments, yet in the lapse of ages might produce by its gradual erosion an effect of which it is difficult to judge the amount.[16]

Before Darwin ever landed on the Galápagos Islands he had already rejected the truth about origins revealed in the Word of God and as a disciple of Lyell was well prepared to apply the uniformitarian principles of slow, gradual geological change over millions of years to the question of biological origins. He was not an unbiased pursuer of truth. Rather, the assumptions based in his anti-biblical, naturalistic worldview controlled his interpretations of what he saw in the world.[17]

TERRY MORTENSON

14 Barlow, *Autobiography of Charles Darwin,* p. 77.

15 Ibid, p. 293.

16 Charles R. Darwin, *Journal of researches into the natural history . . . during the voyage of H.M.S. Beagle* (London: John Murray, 1845), p. 181 (journal entry for 26 April 1834).

17 For a good understanding of the origin of the idea of millions of years of geological history, see Terry Mortenson, *The Great Turning Point: The Church's Catastrophic Mistake on Geology — Before Darwin* (Green Forest, AR: Master Books, 2004) and Terry Mortenson's DVD lecture "Millions of Years: Where Did the Idea Come From?"

CHARLES DARWIN GOT his first glimpse of the Galápagos Islands on September 15, 1835. Little did he know at the time that his name and these islands would be forever associated.

While the concept of biological evolution (molecules-to-man) is believed to be the result of Darwin's observations on these islands, his initial interest in the Galápagos concerned their geology. In fact, the majority of Darwin's notes throughout the entire voyage of the *Beagle* were geological in nature.

Based on their volcanic nature and their distance from the mainland, Darwin reasoned that the islands were never part of the continental landmass and must be relatively young from a geologic standpoint. He was anxious to study the islands and understand their origin.

49

Blue-footed booby

Red-footed booby

In addition to his geologic curiosities, Darwin did, indeed, want to understand the biology of the islands. He wanted to know how plants and animals colonized new islands, and where better to study this than the Galápagos?

As he explored Chatham (modern-day San Cristóbal Island) and several of the other islands, he encountered an amazing variety of animals. He found red and blue-footed boobies. He was fascinated by the iguanas and recorded their behavior and feeding habits. He watched the great tortoises.

It was on James Island (modern day Santiago Island) that he came upon the creature that more than any other is linked with him to this day: the finches. He had already taken a few specimens of birds from other islands, but on James he noted feeding patterns and the variety of beak shapes among these birds. He took many specimens to study on his return to England. Many today refer to these birds as "Darwin's finches."

Hood mockingbird

Contrary to popular mythology, Darwin did not have an epiphany while on the Galápagos. He did observe amazing creatures. He did note variety in beak shapes and tortoise shells. But it was not until a few years later, after his return to England, that he embarked on an extensive examination of the specimens he sent back home.

But is this really the issue? Were the specimens Darwin collected on the Galápagos the basis of what we now call evolution? The simple answer is no.

The primary issue is what Darwin believed prior to visiting the Galápagos. Darwin brought with him on board the *Beagle* the book *Principles of Geology* by Charles Lyell. Lyell set forth the idea that slow geologic changes over vast periods of time produced the earth as we see it today. In other words, Lyell promoted the idea that instead of an earth that was drastically re-shaped by the biblical, global Flood, small changes at a uniform rate over millions of years produced the geology we see today.

Darwin rejected the history in the Bible and accepted the secular concepts of millions of years. Ultimately, it was this belief that led to his conclusions about the samples and specimens he collected on his voyage. This was the framework within which he made his interpretations. It was not really about the evidence; it was about how Darwin interpreted the evidence.

TOMMY MITCHELL

YOUNG DARWIN SAW the striking variation in color, size, form, and behavior among creatures that still awe visitors to Galápagos today. But a much more sinister observation later became the cornerstone of his book *Origin of Species* — the horror of death and the ceaseless struggle for survival.

Even today, Galápagos researchers watch birds and other predators gobble up sea turtles hatching from eggs in beach sand. Only a few reach the sea and predators beneath the waves quickly eat most of those. Only a small percentage of each sea turtle generation survives to later lay eggs on the beach — unwittingly planting a food crop for another generation of predators!

Green sea turtle tracks

Blue heron eating young green sea turtle

Calling it "the war of nature,"[18] Darwin made struggle and death an impersonal, creative force — a substitute for God that could produce higher, more complex animals from a few lower, less complex ancestors.

Despite the profound impact of his evolutionary view, Darwin's observations are easy to describe and to repeat. He noted, for example, that birds in the finch family came in varieties (or species) with variation in beak size. He noted further that varieties with different specific features were often found in different environments. Darwin had seen variation in beak sizes among finches in South America and he knew that floating vegetation mats could transport animals. So, reasoned Darwin, the varied species of finches living among the Galápagos environments originated (descended) from finch populations moving into new places.

Ironically, what Darwin actually saw in God's world (observational science) fits very well with the biblical record of God's acts in history and the scientific models we develop based on that starting point (historical science). Genesis 1 records God's creation of numerous kinds of organisms with the inference that they were to reproduce after their kind. The potential for variation and adaptability built into the ancestors of the dog, horse, cat, and cattle kinds becomes quickly visible through domestic breeding and through migrating animals filling varied environments (as a trip to the Galápagos will illustrate!). In ways biblical creationists already understood, Darwin's observational science helps to explain how and where species survive — but offers no support for the evolution of all life from a common ancestor.

The biblical record of God's acts in history, however, reveals that struggle and death were not present in God's original Edenic creation. Struggle and death entered history only after sin. Scientists have also discovered that Darwin's "god," the "war of nature, from famine and death,"[19] makes things worse, not better, explaining not the origin of new and improved species but rather the origin of defects, disease, and decline.

God's Word is the sure guide to understanding God's world — not only its present and past but also its future. Darwin's followers and others choosing to look at earth history apart from God's Word can only see millions of years of struggle and death until death wins. Those with eyes, hearts, and minds willing to look through biblical glasses see that life wins, new life — rich and abundant through Christ Jesus. His first coming conquered the sting of struggle and death; His coming again establishes a new heaven and earth in which righteousness dwells (2 Peter 3).

GARY PARKER

53

Galápagos finch

18 Charles Darwin, *The Origin of Species*, 6th ed., 1872 (Cricket House Publishers, 2010), p. 336.

19 Ibid, p. 336.

EVOLUTIONISTS TEACH THAT death is a natural part of life. It is by death that the weaker varieties of life are eliminated, allowing the stronger, more adapted organisms to thrive. The only impetus for organisms to evolve in their environment is the threat of death. Without death, we are told that evolution cannot happen and human beings would not exist. As evolutionists see it, we owe our lives to death because death is the driving force behind evolution.

The biblical creationist view is the opposite. The Bible teaches that death was not a part of the original creation, but was introduced as punishment for rebellion against God (Genesis 2:17). Pain and suffering were included in this curse (Genesis 3:14–19). Death and suffering are intruders in a world that was originally perfect (Genesis 1:31, Romans 8:20–21). Death is the logical consequence of our rejection of God, who is life (John 14:6). Death is not our Creator; it is our enemy (1 Corinthians 15:26). In His earthly ministry, Jesus certainly did not see death and suffering as "good." Jesus healed the sick and resurrected the dead. He ultimately conquered death.

Which of these two views is consistent with our experiences in the world? Is death the hero that drives the marvelous diversity of life we find on earth today as evolutionists teach? Or is death an enemy that destroys and brings nothing but pain as the Bible teaches?

Even those people who profess to believe in evolution seem to resist death and suffering as if these were enemies. Evolutionists will take medication when sick, rather than allowing themselves to die and make way for a more evolved creature. An evolutionist will attend the funeral of a friend and will express great sorrow. But if evolution were really true, how would these actions make sense?

The Bible has the answer. It explains in Romans 1:18–20 that the living God has made Himself known to all people in such a way that they cannot escape the truth of creation:

> For the wrath of God is revealed from heaven against all ungodliness and unrighteousness of men, who suppress the truth in unrighteousness, because what may be known of God is manifest in them, for God has shown it to them. For since the creation of the world His invisible attributes are clearly seen, being understood by the things that are made, even His eternal power and Godhead, so that they are without excuse.

Whale bones

Brown pelican

They suppress that truth in unrighteousness. They suppress it even from themselves. Every evolutionist knows in his heart-of-hearts that God is the Creator, and death and suffering are not "good." Evolutionists may deny this with their lips, but their actions show that they know creation to be true. Ultimately, the biblical view of death and suffering is the only view that makes sense.

JASON LISLE

55

WHEN MOST PEOPLE think of Charles Darwin, they think of the word *evolution*. So is that his real legacy? I suggest not.

When people think of Darwin, they also think of the Galápagos Islands and Darwin's finches? Could that be his real legacy? Not at all.

What about the term *natural selection?* Isn't that so closely associated with Charles Darwin that this must be his legacy? I say no. Then what about his book *Origin of Species* — surely that must be his legacy? But I say that is not so.

I suggest that the real legacy of Charles Darwin could be summed up in this one verse of Scripture:

> In those days there was no king in Israel; everyone did what was right in his own eyes.

> —Judges 21:25

We live in an era of history when we see moral relativism permeating the Western world. We see increasing acceptance of gay marriage, abortion, euthanasia, and many other social ills.

So is Darwin the cause of such moral relativism? No. From a biblical perspective, sin is the root cause of these moral evils. But nonetheless, I suggest that there is a connection between Darwin and the moral relativism that pervades our culture today — and I insist that this is Darwin's real legacy.

Darwin popularized an idea to explain how the diversity of life could supposedly arise by natural processes. Thus, what Darwin really did was to popularize a belief about the origin of living things without God! We need to understand the consequences of such a belief in naturalism. If there is no God, and human beings are the result of such natural processes as Darwin proposed, then humans are really no different than animals.

If we are just animals and there is no God, then from such an atheistic evolutionist perspective, if we put down unwanted cats, why not put down unwanted kids in their mother's wombs. Life is truly a purposeless existence.

What Darwin did is summarized in these verses from Romans 1:

> . . . and changed the glory of the incorruptible God into an image made like corruptible man — and birds and four-footed animals and creeping things. . . . who exchanged the truth of God for the lie, and worshiped and served the creature rather than the Creator, who is blessed forever. Amen.

> —Romans 1:23–25

Darwinian evolution makes the creature the creator, as man believes the "lie" that life made itself and that it is not the result of the creative processes of an infinite God.

Darwin's real legacy is that he popularized a philosophy to explain life by natural processes. In a world of people who have inherited the sin nature of Adam, many continue in their rebellion against the God of creation. They have determined (falsely) in their own minds that God and His Word are not true and do whatever is right in their own eyes.

Yes — I suggest that is the real legacy of Charles Darwin.

KEN HAM

56

"Where were you when I laid the foundations of the earth?
Tell Me, if you have understanding."

—Job 38:4

57

TO HOLD DARWINIAN thinking to its most consistent end, the gospel must be robbed of its power. Paul stated:

"For Christ did not send me to baptize but to preach the gospel, and not with words of eloquent wisdom, lest the cross of Christ be emptied of its power."

—1 Corinthians 1:17; ESV

This is not that the success and power of Christ's sacrifice or God's sovereignty is somehow incomplete. On the contrary, Paul is saying that when men follow men, we fall into error and can end up following a gospel message robbed of its richness and possibly even saving power.

The foundational elements of evolutionary philosophies and the Word of God are diametrically opposed to each other. Genesis 1:26 makes it very clear that mankind was created in the image of God. Darwin proposed that "races" of people evolved at different periods of times with some closer to their ape-like ancestors than others.

Being specially created as God's image bearers is no small detail when it comes to the gospel message. Mankind was created to bear the light of the glory of God as they filled the earth in obedience and worship of their Creator. We were to subdue the earth and have dominion over all living creatures. But we failed.

Instead of having dominion over all living creatures, Adam and Eve submitted to one of these very creatures when they were tempted by the serpent and ate the forbidden fruit. They had exchanged the glory of God for a lie (Romans 1:22–23). The biblical account of man's position is clear. Because we all come from one set of parents who were specially created in the image of God, we are all bound in their identity. "Therefore, just as through one man sin entered the world, and death through sin, and thus death spread to all men, because all sinned" (Romans 5:12). A consistent evolutionary belief system disregards image bearing and deems human failure as inconsequential.

If the beginning of the Genesis narrative is changed to replace

Multiple rock layers exposed by erosion on Santiago

The mountains melt like wax at the presence of the LORD,
At the presence of the Lord of the whole earth.

—Psalm 97:5

Bartolomé landscape with Pinnacle Rock

specially created image bearers with Darwin's philosophy of human origins, the most consistent result is a change to the gospel message. If mankind was evolved from ape-like creatures over different times it is not only impossible to say whom the sinners are, it is also impossible to define sin. The biblical position is clear in that without Christ every human being remains under the judgment of God and is in desperate need of a Savior (John 3:36). Jesus as the second Adam is the only key to our salvation. Yet we need not even be concerned if humanity is just another evolved animal.

Jesus came as the only human to perfectly bear the image of God. When Adam failed and submitted to the serpent in a perfect paradise, Christ overcame Satan's temptations in a sin-corrupted world. Christ is the true image bearer of God's glory who, as the promised Seed of the woman, has crushed the head of the serpent (Genesis 3:15, Hebrews 1:3).

In Christ alone there is a special hope. "Just as we have borne the image of the man of dust, we shall also bear the image of the man of heaven" (1 Corinthians 15:49; ESV). In Christ Jesus we will again one day be eternally restored to the image bearers we were meant to be.

While there are people who hold to a Darwinian view of origins and the gospel of Christ, they do so inconsistently and are at great risk of robbing the gospel message of its power. Taken to the logical conclusion, Darwinian thinking eliminates the need for a gospel, and robs humanity of the hope in being eternally restored to bearing the image of our Creator, Jesus Christ. It is the foundational history in Genesis that provides not just an account of origins but also an anchor of hope. Because humanity is created in the image of God in Eden there is a historical reference point for a true restoration of image bearing in Jesus Christ.

STEVE HAM

The animals and plants of the Galápagos are definitely its most spectacular feature. Before going to the Galápagos Islands, I had never attempted any type of wildlife photography (unless you count taking pictures of animals at the zoo!). But the animals have no fear of people so it was possible for me to get close and take the amazing pictures you see throughout this book.

The relationship between man and animals on the islands hearkens back to the Garden of Eden before sin and death entered the world — when man lived in perfect harmony with the animals. One day when we were in the Galápagos, we took a panga (rubber raft) ride into a protected cove near Floreana where many young sea lions played. They dove under our boats and swam alongside us. When we landed on the island, the sea lions came up onto the shore as if to say, "Where are you going? We were having fun!"

Another highlight of the trip was an amazing aerial display by the blue-footed boobies. As we came around a corner in Black Turtle

Galápagos sea lions

Cove off the coast of Santa Cruz, there were hundreds of blue-footed boobies floating on the water. Within moments, as if responding to some unknown signal, they all took flight, flew a short circle in the air, and then dive-bombed back into the water to capture their prey. Blue-footed boobies hit the water at 60 miles per hour and yet God has designed their heads and bodies to withstand the force of this impact. It was truly incredible to see so many of them diving at once!

However, on the Galápagos Islands there were also vivid reminders of the Fall. One evening a student used a flashlight to spot an eight-to-nine foot shark in the water. Minutes later, a large sea lion hopped up on the back of our ship. He was missing part of a fin and bleeding. There was really nothing we could do for the sea lion and minutes later he rolled off the deck and back into the ocean. We can only guess if he was able to escape further injury from the shark. On Santiago, as we observed green sea turtle nests, a Galápagos mockingbird flew in on top of the nest. The mockingbird was scratching at the sand in the nests to "help" the young sea turtles

Hood mockingbird

make their way to the surface so it could eat them. Events like these made me long for the consummation when all things will be restored to perfection, including the relationship between man and animals (Isaiah 11:6–8).

Charles Darwin likely observed similar events in the Galápagos but came to very different conclusions. Darwin didn't believe that the Bible, especially the Old Testament, recorded true history. He couldn't reconcile the existence of a good God and the cruelty and destruction he saw in nature because he didn't believe in the historical account of the Fall in Genesis. Although he observed the amazing diversity of animals such as the iguana, finch, tortoise, and blue-footed booby, he didn't believe that God had created the ancestors of these animals on Days 5 and 6 of creation week (Genesis 1:20–25) because he didn't believe in the historical account of creation in Genesis. Based on man's ideas about

the past apart from God and His Word, Darwin developed and popularized the idea that all living creatures — both past and present — descended from a simple common ancestor over millions of years of evolution by natural selection (historical science).

There is no doubt that living things have changed over time, but to what extent is really the question. God's Word is true and there are certain biological principles given in Scripture. In addition, creation scientists have developed models based on the Bible to understand and explain how animals and plants have changed over time (historical science). As we will see, observational science (science we do today) confirms and is consistent with the biological principles in God's Word and the models based on His Word. Observational science does not confirm and is inconsistent with molecules-to-man evolution. This is not to say that creation scientists are perfect and have all the

Lava lizard

Female frigate bird with young chick

62

answers, but we are more likely to arrive at the correct answers because we start with the inerrant Word of God and thus the truth about the past.

According to Scripture, God created animals according to their kind (Genesis 1:21, 24). What is a "kind"? Creation scientists believe that an animal "kind" is equivalent to the family level (with exceptions) in modern classification schemes (Kingdom-Phylum-Class-Order-**Family**-Genus-Species). The inference from Scripture is that animals were to reproduce according to their kind. This is clearly seen in the account of Noah's Flood where Noah is told to take two of every kind (and seven of some) air-breathing, land-dwelling animals aboard the ark (Genesis 6:20). The idea was to keep those animal kinds alive so they could multiply and fill the earth after the Flood (Genesis 8:17). If one kind of animal could evolve into a different kind of animal then there would be no need to preserve all the air-breathing, land-dwelling kinds.

Most animals within a family may breed with each other and produce offspring. For example, zebras and horses are in the same family (Equidae) and can breed and produce a zorse. These types of animals are called hybrids and they typically exhibit characteristics of both parents. Since animals within a family may breed with each other and produce offspring, this is believed to be the level of the kind for most animals. Creationists also use the word *baramin* as a synonym for "kind." Baramin comes from two Hebrew words — *bara* meaning "created" and *min* meaning "kind," thus "created kind."

In our present world, we observe that animals reproduce according to their kinds. Dogs produce dogs, cats produce cats, and so on. Some might claim that we don't observe one animal kind evolving into other animal kinds, as molecules-to-man evolution proposes, because we only observe animals over a short period of time. Biological evolution requires millions and billions of years to achieve this supposed change. But time is really not the issue. Time is useless if there is no biological mechanism by which these changes can occur. No matter how many times you roll a six-sided die, you will never roll an eight.

Evolutionists believe that the mechanisms of mutation and natural selection lead to the gain of new structures and functions necessary

for one kind of animal to evolve into a different kind of animal. For example, a dinosaur can't evolve into a bird unless it gains the ability to make feathers. Mutations, changes in DNA, are believed to add to or alter the DNA to produce these new structures and functions, but observational science does not support this claim. Instead, mutations are either nearly neutral (making no change in the organism) or are destructive (damaging the DNA and harming the organism). Mutations have never been observed to add or alter DNA to cause the formation of new structures and functions of the type necessary for one kind of organism to evolve into a different kind.

Natural selection is defined as "the process by which individuals possessing a set of traits that confer a survival advantage in a given environment tend to leave more offspring on average that survive to reproduce in the next generation."[1] Changes in the beak size

Galápagos penguin

---

1   Roger Patterson, *Evolution Exposed: Biology* (Green Forest, AR: Master Books, 2009), p. 58.

Galápagos finch

Blue-footed boobies in flight

of Darwin's finches are a great example of how natural selection works. Beak size (within a species) is dependent on factors like food availability related to the weather extremes commonly occurring in the Galápagos. Finches with large beaks are more likely to survive (and subsequently reproduce) when the major food source is large seeds. Those with small beaks have a difficult time breaking apart the large seeds and are less likely to survive (and reproduce). Thus, a greater number of birds in the next generation have large beaks. When the major food source changes to small seeds, the opposite is true and birds with smaller beaks survive better and the predominant beak size in the following generation is smaller.

Although the average beak size may increase or decrease, the beaks never become anything other than a beak! Natural selection can only select from structures and functions already present in the organism, not create new ones. Neither mutations nor natural selection result in directional changes that allow organisms to evolve into different kinds of organisms regardless of how much time is available.

But if all the animals in the past and present descended from the original animal kinds that God created, what accounts for such great diversity? Both creationists and evolutionists believe mechanisms such as mutation, natural selection, genetic drift, and others can lead to speciation (changes within a kind or family), because this is what we observe happening today. We have many different breeds of dogs, but they are all still dogs. Creationists and evolutionists differ as to the effects these various mechanisms can produce over time, but not because of the actual, observed evidence. The evidence is clear — there is no biological mechanism to gain new structures and function to change one kind of animal into a different kind. Rather, the difference is the interpretation of the evidence based on our starting point — do we start with God's Word or man's ideas apart from God about the past as we interpret the evidence?

Although God's original creation was "very good" (Genesis 1:31), He foreknew that Adam and Eve would sin and that all living things would be cursed as part of His punishment for sin (Genesis 3). This event is known as the Fall of mankind. God had to punish sin because He is holy and just, but He is also gracious, loving, compassionate, and merciful. He provided a Redeemer for mankind through His Son Jesus Christ (Genesis 3:15; John 3:16). He also cares for the animals and plants He created (Luke 12:24) and equipped them with biological mechanisms to change, adapt, and survive in a world suffering under the effects of the Curse.

Many creation scientists believe that certain adaptive traits of organisms may be the result of mediated design. Several creation scientists described it this way:

God specifically designed the created kinds with genes [in the DNA] that could be turned on to help them adapt to new environments. In other words, the Creator continues to accomplish His purpose for organisms after creation, not by creating something new, but by working through existing parts that were designed during Creation Week. An analogy is the manufacturer of a fully equipped Swiss army knife, who stores within the knife every tool a camper might need as he faces the unknown challenges of wilderness living.[2]

God designed these adaptive traits to be expressed only under certain conditions to allow animals and plants to survive in a post-Fall world. For example, the original iguana ancestor that arrived on the Galápagos Islands may not have been able to forage in the ocean for food. But certain environmental cues, such as the scarcity of food on the volcanic landscape, may have triggered the expression of genes already present in the DNA of the iguanas (nothing new) to allow them to feed in the water. Over time this may have led to speciation — the marine iguana species became distinct from the original land iguana ancestor on the islands so that there were two species where there was once only one. But they were still iguanas. Mediated design may also be a factor that led to the flightless Galápagos cormorant and speciation in *Scalesia* (Galápagos sunflower trees) and *Opuntia* (prickly pear cactus). Understanding the God-designed mechanisms that result in adaptation and speciation is an active area of research for creation scientists.

Just as God cares for His creation, as God's image bearers we are to care for it, too. God commanded Adam and Eve, "Be fruitful and multiply; fill the earth and subdue it; have dominion over the fish of the sea, over the birds of the air, and over every living thing that moves on the earth" (Genesis 1:28). This dominion was not to be harsh and cruel but rather loving and kind as God is in His dominion over us.

Conservation is a major concern on the Galápagos Islands as both intentional and careless acts in the past have led to great damage of the islands' ecosystems. From the 1600s to the 1800s, pirates and those involved in the whaling industry took thousands and thousands of

2   Tom Hennigan, Georgia Purdom, and Todd Charles Wood, "Creation's Hidden Potential," *Answers*, January–March 2009, p. 70–75.

65

tortoises from the islands for food aboard their ships. In addition, feral animals (domesticated animals that have escaped into the wild) such as goats, pigs, and dogs, eat tortoise eggs, making it nearly impossible for some tortoise species to reproduce without assistance. The Charles Darwin Research Station on Santa Cruz has a large tortoise-breeding program that helps reintroduce and maintain tortoises on certain islands where they are endangered. These types of programs help not only the animals but also the people that live on the islands and depend on ecotourism for their livelihood.

The flora and fauna of the Galápagos Islands are a beautiful picture of both the majesty of God in His creation and the mercy of God in

Prickly pear cactus

a fallen world. Many people have asked me, "If the evidence against molecules-to-man evolution is clear, why do people still believe this false idea?" We need to understand that this is not an issue of the evidence but an issue of the heart. The Apostle Paul, in Romans 1:18–25 is clear — people know the truth of a Creator God but suppress that knowledge in unrighteousness. People know that if evolution is not true, then God is real and is in authority over them. Many willfully choose to continue in their sin, rebel against their Creator, and this will ultimately lead them to hell. The choice to believe God exists and receive Christ as Savior so we can spend eternity with Him can only be made on earth in this life (Hebrews 9:27–28). What choice will you make?

Marine iguanas

THE BLUE-FOOTED BOOBY is the most "entertaining" and well-known bird on the Galápagos Islands. It is in the bird family Sulidae along with five other species of boobies. All six species are in the genus *Sula,* indicating close relationship among the species. There has even been hybridization between some of the species in this family (among masked, brown, and red-footed boobies), but there are no known hybrids between the blue-footed booby and any other species in the genus *Sula.*

Approximately half of all breeding pairs of blue-footed boobies nest in the Galápagos Islands. The most conspicuous feature of adults of this species is their intense blue feet. Studies have shown that the bluer the feet in both sexes, the more attractive they are to one another.

A natural question that comes to mind when watching these birds is, "What makes their feet blue?" The blue color is produced by a combination of carotenoids (fat-soluble pigments in plants and animals) and structural color, which is produced by the reflection and refraction of light as it strikes the feet. The carotenoids, which are obtained from their diet, also provide antioxidants and stimulants to strengthen their immune systems.

Foot color is also an accurate indicator of a booby's level of nourishment, which in turn can affect the success of chick rearing. Chicks raised by fathers with bright feet grow faster than chicks raised by fathers with dull feet.

The courtship ritual of the male blue-footed booby is inextricably linked to its blue feet. He displays them to his prospective mate by strutting in front of her, conspicuously lifting one and then the other foot to impress her. Nest material is then picked up in the beak and offered to her, after which he engages in another foot-strutting display.

The bond between the two is reinforced throughout the nesting season by a dance that includes sky-pointing, the male facing his mate and lifting his head and beak skyward while keeping his wings and tail raised. Also, both sexes have a peculiar aerial greeting in which an incoming bird stretches its conspicuous blue feet forward before landing at the nest site.

It is obvious that there is much more meaning to the blue foot color of the blue-footed booby than just "pretty feet." The God of the Bible created these birds with amazing variation in the DNA of their original kind to allow for adaptations, in part due to geographic isolation (like on the Galápagos Islands), which resulted in the appearance of different species of boobies within their created kind.

DONNA O'DANIEL

67

CORMORANTS ARE A type of sea bird found throughout the world. There are 40 different species of cormorants likely descended and diversified from a single created cormorant kind. The Galápagos Islands of Isabela and Fernandina contain a very interesting variant of cormorant that is unique and found nowhere else in the world.

The distinguishing feature of the Galápagos cormorant is the fact that it is flightless. In fact, its wings are about one-third the size of a normal cormorant. This inability to fly, however, provides an advantage that facilitates its feeding and foraging behavior in the ocean. The short wings act like lateral fins and aid in the diving and maneuverability of the bird underwater as it snaps up fish and other aquatic prey.

In the Galápagos, there are a few key environmental factors that contribute to the unique advantage of being flightless. First, there are no large predators on the islands. Without pressure from predators, there is no need for the birds to fly off and escape. Second, the beaches of the Galápagos are easily navigated by walking. As a result, birds don't have to fly to reach their nesting sites like most of their relatives that live on cliff-like ocean shores.

Interestingly, DNA studies have shown that the Galápagos cormorant is most closely related to cormorants on the coast of South America. The first cormorants to arrive on the islands obviously had larger wings and likely flew to the Galápagos from the main continent.

So the key question is, how was this unique variant of cormorant able to diversify from its longer-winged, flying ancestors? There are two possible answers to this question. The first is that enough genetic variation was built into the original created cormorant gene pool and they just needed the right environment for populations to eventually develop in which that trait would be expressed and then become predominant (mediated design).

A second idea is that a mutation, which affected the development of the wings and would normally be harmful to a bird, was not a disadvantage to the cormorants. Since food is plentiful in the ocean and there are few predators on the islands, wings for flight are not necessary. Although the mutations may have resulted in diminished wing development, it was not a disadvantage to the cormorants because of the unique Galápagos environment.

Clearly, the Galápagos cormorants display the amazing bio-engineering and creativity of the Creator and the incredible ability of His created creatures to fill and adapt to a wide diversity of ecological niches.

JEFFREY TOMKINS

68

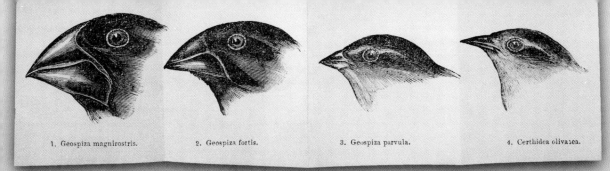

1. Geospiza magnirostris.   2. Geospiza fortis.   3. Geospiza parvula.   4. Certhidea olivacea.

A SMALL OUTDOOR laboratory — the Galápagos Islands — has provided a glimpse into the process of speciation that has been operating in the millennia since the Flood. Specifically, the changes observed in the finches that are native to these islands (Darwin's finches) have revealed fascinating insights into the mechanisms by which species arose from the "kinds" on board the ark.

Recent studies have established the ancestry of the 14 species on the Galápagos. Hybridization between two individuals identifies members of a common kind, and a recent finch and sparrow breeding investigation suggested that upward of 1,000 species of birds belong to this kind, including the Galápagos finches.

The common heritage of these finches enlarges the explanatory task for the biblical creation model. Since differences in beak size and shape are distinguishing traits in these 14 species, the process of speciation post-Flood must have involved anatomical changes in bird bills. How did this occur?

The "blueprint" for beak formation — the DNA in each finch species — appears to be modular. Making a few minor modifications to the original modular blueprint is a fast and efficient way to make changes in an anatomical structure. Recently, scientists have been able to modify these modules in DNA to produce dramatic differences in beak size and shape. The actions of just two genes — *BMP4* (bone morphogenetic protein 4) and calmodulin — appear to be sufficient to produce the large variety in finch beak depth, length, and width. These results confirm the feasibility of producing many finch species

after the Flood from a few ancestors on the ark.

But there are limits to the process of speciation and anatomical change. Evolution requires not only changes in finch beaks, but also changes that eventually resulted in dinosaurs evolving into birds! Unfortunately for Darwin, we have never observed this. Why not? Imagine the difficulty difficulty of converting a sedan, step-by-step, into an airplane. It would be impractical to try to create blueprints for a Boeing 747 jumbo jet from modifications of the car blueprints. Instead, a whole new plan would be required.

Conversely, in the biological world, dramatic differences in the blueprints of each kind are seen early in development. Shortly after sperm meets egg and the new embryo begins dividing and growing, obvious differences are seen among the different classes of animals. God seems to have placed fundamentally different developmental programs in different kinds of creatures, which cannot be interconverted by slow modification of individual steps. No wonder evolution has yet to be observed!

Darwin's finches elegantly illustrate the feasibility of many new species forming after the Flood from a few kinds of animals on the ark. Thus, when Darwin passed through the Galápagos, he didn't observe a textbook example of evolution; he observed the handiwork of God!

NATHANIEL JEANSON

EVOLUTION IN ACTION!

That is the claim of the authors of many books, including science textbooks, concerning the finches that live on the Galápagos Islands. While on the islands, Darwin collected samples of the finches. The variation in the beaks became an important part of his explanation for the evolutionary change (from molecules-to-man) he later proposed. Peter and Rosemary Grant, who spent many decades carefully studying the finch populations of the Galápagos, expanded on his observations beginning in the 1970s.

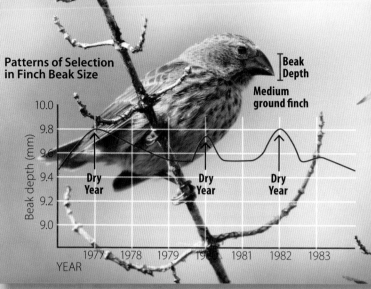

Patterns of Selection in Finch Beak Size

Beak Depth

Medium ground finch

Beak depth (mm)

10.0 / 9.8 / 9.6 / 9.4 / 9.2 / 9.0

Dry Year / Dry Year / Dry Year

YEAR / 1977 / 1978 / 1979 / 1980 / 1981 / 1982 / 1983

Adapted from Campbell, N., B. Williamson, and R. Heyden, *Biology: Exploring Life* (Florida Teacher's Edition), Pearson Prentice Hall, Upper Saddle River, New Jersey, 2006, p. 316.

The variation in the beaks of Darwin's finches seems to be a favorite piece of evidence of the writers of high school biology textbooks. The units on evolution often feature pictures of the finches as well as cameos of the Grants. In his book *Ecology and Evolution of Darwin's Finches,* Peter Grant lays out the explanation for how the Galápagos finches evolved over hundreds of thousands of years from an ancestor that migrated from the mainland of South America, where similar species are found.

While the careful and thoughtful work that the Grants have done in examining the finches can be applauded, the interpretations of the data they have gathered are another story. The textbooks repeat this interpretation often using graphs, like the one on this page, to show the changes in beak size as evidence for evolution. But look a bit more closely at the graph. There is no net change! Sure, the size of the beaks changes in response to the weather patterns, but beak size returns to the baseline when the weather returns to normal.

The textbooks use this fluctuation in beak size to explain the observable process of natural selection. But then they take the observable evidence and use it to support the unobservable idea of large-scale changes needed for evolution. There is no doubt that the changes seen in the finches are an example of creatures adapting to their changing environment, but is this evolution in action?

Natural selection can only act on traits an organism already possesses — it selects from what is already present. The idea that birds evolved from dinosaurs requires dinosaurs to gain a lot of new traits such as feathers. How does a process that selects from what is already present in an organism cause the organism to gain new traits? Well, it can't!

While the Grants' research helps us to understand how God has created these finches with the ability to adapt to their changing environment (natural selection and adaptation), it has no power to explain how dinosaurs turned into birds (evolution). We can only truly understand the creation when we begin our thinking with the revelation the Creator has given us in His Word. God created animals according to their kind, and they reproduce according to their kind. Darwin, the Grants, and the textbook authors cannot lead us to an understanding of the truth when they begin with ideas which are contrary to what God has revealed in the Bible.

ROGER PATTERSON

WHEN DARWIN VISITED the Galápagos Islands, he observed the only species of marine iguana in the world. He was impressed with its diving abilities but not its looks, calling them "imps of darkness." Iguanas are reptiles and reptiles are cold-blooded, meaning they cannot generate their own body heat. Nevertheless, the marine iguana survives and obtains food from the cold waters surrounding the Galápagos, eating mainly algae on rocky shores. Adults may even dive 50 feet or more in search of food. What is the origin of this unique animal? Many believe the marine iguana descended from the land iguana by evolving new features needed for life in the water over long spans of time. However, there is no biological mechanism for animals to gain these new traits. An alternative explanation for the different features of marine and land iguanas is mediated design.

The marine iguana *(Amblyrhynchus cristatus)* has salt glands for ejecting excess salt from its body when it swallows seawater. However, this is not a brand new feature as the Galápagos land iguana *(Conolophus subcristatus)* also has salt glands, but they are less developed than the salt glands in marine iguanas. From a biblical creation perspective, this feature of the marine iguana may be an example of mediated design. In other words, the original iguana kind was created with the genetic information (in the DNA) for salt glands. This information was more robustly expressed at a later time in an appropriate (salty) environment, allowing greater development of salt glands and a greater ability of iguanas to survive and obtain food from the ocean (as in the case of marine iguanas today). God cares for His

Marine iguana with lava lizard on head

creation and He designed animals with the ability to adapt to varying environments. This ability may have been especially important following the Flood.

In addition, the salt glands appear not to have evolved from an ancestral organ of one common ancestor of all reptiles, as evolutionary ideas would predict. Instead, the salt glands of the marine iguana, and many other lizards, are nasal glands, whereas sea turtles use slightly modified tear duct glands and crocodiles use tongue glands. Though there are exceptions, this is consistent with the biblical concept of created kinds. The original individuals of each of these kinds of reptiles (e.g., lizards, turtles, and crocodiles) possessed different types of salt glands because they are distinct created kinds.

The marine iguana also has long, strong claws that allow it to hold on to rocks in the water as it eats, instead of being swept away by currents. Land iguanas have claws too, but they are shorter and weaker than those of the marine iguana. This is likely another example of mediated design. The original iguana kind was created with genetic information for claws. This information would be robustly expressed in the future in an appropriate environment, allowing long, strong claws to develop for holding on to rocks as it obtained food from the water. These types of changes may have led to speciation within the iguana kind, but not iguanas evolving into a different kind of animal over long spans of time.

Furthermore, the existence and abundance of numerous hybrid iguanas all over the world (including hybrids of Galápagos marine and land iguanas) points to all of them having descended from the same created iguana kind. This finding is very consistent with and gives support for the biblical inference that God created animals to reproduce according to their kind versus the evolutionary idea of one kind of animal evolving into a different kind of animal.

DOUG OLIVER

72

Land iguana

Marine iguana

EVER SINCE THE discovery of the Galápagos Islands, the giant tortoises have loomed large not only on the landscape but also on maritime history, science, and ecotourism. Many men who frequented the islands (particularly whalers) began noticing the differences between tortoises on different islands as well as different populations on the same islands. The whaling industry was in full swing in the 1800s, and during much of that century (and the centuries before) tens of thousands of tortoises were taken on board ship alive and slaughtered for meat when needed. As a result, observant men could guess with some degree of accuracy what island a particular tortoise was from by its size, shape, color, and other subtleties (even taste!). Biologists have long since taken over the job of detailed descriptions and have attempted to explain how those differences arose. These differences fall well within the variations that can occur within a created kind (or baramin).

The current ballpark estimate of the total number of Galápagos tortoise subspecies

Domed Galápagos tortoise

Saddleback Galápagos tortoise

that have lived on the islands is between 10 and 15. Unfortunately, several of these subspecies have gone extinct due to overharvesting, land settlement, agriculture, and the introduction of competitive or destructive mammals. The most obvious difference between the populations is the shape of the upper shell, or carapace. There is the smaller saddleback tortoise, the larger domed tortoise, and sizes between those two.

It is largely conjecture what the first tortoises that came to these islands looked like. Were they saddleback, domed, or intermediate between the two? Were they large or small? If they were something like the previously assumed closest relative, the Chaco Tortoise of South America, they were small and domed. However, new genetic evidence suggests that they are more closely related to African hinge-backed tortoises, which are also small and low-domed. It's possible that their ancestors (regardless of where they came from) were also giants that went extinct on the mainland after their descendants had colonized these islands.

There is some evidence that the saddleback tortoises are more associated with lower elevation islands and that domed tortoises are more associated with higher elevation islands. While this seems to be a general pattern (with exceptions) it doesn't explain why those different shapes arose in the first place. Some biologists speculate that the saddleback shape arose because some islands have tree-like prickly pear cactuses. As the story goes, those tortoises with longer necks and shells hitched up higher in the front had an advantage over those who didn't because they were more successful at reaching the prickly salad bar. Presumably, they survived and passed on their saddleback genes to the next generation. The problem with this scenario is that there isn't just tall prickly pear cactus where the saddlebacks live. In fact, there is often low-growing prickly pear cactus on islands that are home to saddlebacks. Another explanation is that the saddleback shape arose because male tortoises competing for females display their dominance by lifting their heads up high. The higher-reaching males usually win mating rights and pass their "higher-reaching" genes to their offspring.

These theories might offer a possible explanation if habitats were strongly correlated with shell shape, but the locations of these differently shaped tortoises don't neatly match up with the habitats that are thought to produce them. Since we can't observe the past and there is no record of the history of these tortoises, we need to humbly admit that we may never be certain how these different shapes came about even if there is some truth to these theories.

GORDON WILSON

74

Mangroves with exposed roots at low tide

ORGANISMS ARE AMAZINGLY designed for dealing with the harsh and varied environmental conditions of the Galápagos Islands. Walking along the coastal zones of many islands, I encountered dense tangles of beautiful trees whose roots penetrated lava rock and were submerged in saltwater. The trees were mangroves, and varieties of creatures both abound and depend on these crucial habitats. The Galápagos is home to four mangrove species — white, red, black, and button — and all have complex systems allowing them to live and reproduce in the harsh environment of saltwater and low oxygen.

Salt can be deadly in large concentrations, and different mangrove species have different ways of dealing with it. For example, the red mangrove prevents salt from entering its cells through a complex "filtering" system, while the black and white mangroves let salt into their tissues but pump it back out through special leaf glands. When leaves drop off, the excess salt goes with them.

Oxygen is another issue for mangroves growing in water. Therefore, they have specialized roots that grow into the air. Some species produce roots that extend from the trunk while others have small roots that come up from under water into the air.

All reproduce using flowers, which produce seeds that stick to the tree. The seeds develop into pods that are resistant to salt and desiccation. They will drop from the tree and either take root or disperse to new locations by water currents and generate new trees. Mangrove forests are a wonderful example of God's design, beauty, and provision for a wide diversity of animals that make the Galápagos their home.

TOM HENNIGAN

THERE ARE NATIVE sunflowers in the Galápagos, but most people would not recognize them as such. First of all, they are not yellow and the flowering heads are not large and nodding. Instead, they are white, and some don't even have the circular row of showy "petals" around the outside of the flowering head. Second, they are not fast-growing summer annuals; they are shrubs and some are even trees! Third, they aren't even in the genus (plural, genera) *Helianthus*, which literally means "sun-flower;" they are in the genus *Scalesia*.

So how do we know they are sunflowers? Conventional classification places *Scalesia* in the same group of similar genera as sunflowers. The genera in this group are on the mainland of South America. Some genera have yellow-, white-, and pink-flowered species. Other genera have species with and without the showy "petals," as well as range in size from small-flowered to medium-flowered, and some genera have both woody and herbaceous species.

In other words, the variation in this group connects the *Scalesia* genus smoothly with the *Helianthus* genus. Creation biologists have examined this variation and have concluded that, indeed, *Scalesia* is in the same created kind as *Helianthus*, and the species of *Scalesia* should be thought of as sunflowers.

Besides the fact that it is amazing that sunflowers can form trees, *Scalesia* is fascinating because the 15 species of *Scalesia* exhibit an amazing range of forms. Three species are present almost exclusively as trees in the higher elevation forests where sufficient rain falls. *Scalesia pedunculata* grows to 30 feet or more and is the most widespread form occurring on at least three major islands. The other two are shorter and grow in separate areas of the two westernmost islands. All the other species are shrubs growing at lower elevations in more desert-like environments.

Evolutionary biologists think of the species of *Scalesia* as an example of adaptive radiation. That is, the ancestor presumably arrived in the Galápagos before the native vegetation became established so that its descendants evolved into diverse species by adapting to the diversity of habitats that they found there. There are two problems for evolutionary theory here. First, the tree species in the moist uplands are distinct from each other and yet they are exposed to essentially the same environmental factors. The same is true for the shrub species in the dry lowlands. This goes for every trait found in each of these species that differentiates it from its neighboring species. How can such varied traits for each species be adaptive if their environment is the same? Second, all or certainly most of these proposed adaptive traits that are supposed to have evolved in *Scalesia* in the Galápagos are actually found scattered in species of the other genera of the sunflower group not on the Galápagos.

However, this situation makes more sense in light of biblical history and creationist models of biological diversity. Creationists hypothesize that God designed the original created kinds with latent genetic information that would become expressed at future times to allow that organisms to diversify in new environments (mediated design). Those future times would hold the new and often stress-filled world that organisms would find in the years following the Flood. The bare volcanic surfaces of the rising Galápagos Islands would be just the sort of harsh habitat that might promote the expression of latent genetic information to produce the unusual forms of otherwise familiar-looking plants.

When viewed through a biblical lens, the species of *Scalesia* declare the glory of God, who judges sin, as He did with the Flood, but who is full of grace in restoring beauty and fullness to that which was marred by sin.

ROGER SANDERS

WHEN FRAY TOMÁS de Berlanga accidentally discovered the Galápagos Islands in March of 1535, the ship's crew, desperate for water in the parched landscape, "resorted to a leaf of some thistles like prickly pears, and because they were somewhat juicy, although not very tasty, we began to eat of them and squeeze them to draw all the water from them."[3] What Berlanga and his men ate is now known as prickly pear, a type of cactus common throughout the Galápagos Islands.

In the Galápagos, prickly pears provide food and water to many of the animal natives. Finches, tortoises, and lava lizards are all known to feast on the pads, flowers, and fruits of prickly pears. Native animals also help the prickly pear complete its life cycle. The cactus finch and carpenter bee are believed to be important pollinators and lava lizards and tortoises are important for dispersing seeds.

The Galápagos prickly pears are classified in the genus *Opuntia*, a group of about 180 cactus species that originally ranged from Argentina to Canada. In the Galápagos, botanists recognized about six *Opuntia* species with very different characteristics. For example, the prickly pears of Genovesa and Marchena are sprawling, shrubby forms called *Opuntia helleri*. Other islands have much taller prickly pears, with central trunks and a crown of pads, much like a tree. The tallest of all Galápagos prickly pears is the *gigantea* variety of *Opuntia echios*, which grows on the southwestern side of Santa Cruz. The *gigantea* variety can tower as high as 36 feet!

Opuntia species are all visually similar to each other and studies of *Opuntia* DNA have confirmed close similarity between Galápagos species and prickly pears from mainland South America. Prickly pears are also known for their ability to hybridize (breed with each other). All of this evidence implies that all 180 prickly pear species belong to the same created kind (or baramin). Since the individual Galápagos species are all similar to each other, their ancestors probably came to the Galápagos in a single colonization event. Some piece of a South American prickly pear came to the islands, either by floating across the open ocean or by traveling as seeds in the intestines of a bird or lizard.

Once in the Galápagos, why did the prickly pears diversify into the forms we find there today? Some have claimed that giant tortoises trying to eat the prickly pear fruit prevented the sprawling forms of *Opuntia* from becoming widespread. In other words, the only prickly pears that could survive on the islands where tortoises live were the tall ones that kept their flowers and fruits out of the reach of the tortoises. A more likely explanation of the diversity of Galápagos prickly pears is competition. Tree-form prickly pears in Galápagos are often just as tall as the trees that grow around them, implying that the prickly pears are competing with other plants for sunlight.

Are the tree-form prickly pears some kind of amazing evolutionary adaptation? That also seems unlikely. The tree-form prickly pear variety can sometimes be found in the same species as the shrubby, sprawling forms. The prickly pear diversity appears to be an outworking of design that God built into the original ancestors of prickly pears.

TODD CHARLES WOOD

3   Joseph R. Slevin, "The Galápagos Islands: A History of Their Exploration,"
Occasional Papers of the California Academy of Sciences 25 (1959): 1–150.

O God, You are my God; early will I seek You; my soul thirsts for You; my flesh longs for You in a dry and thirsty land where there is no water.

—Psalm 63:1

79

THE PRESENT-DAY CREATION is filled with countless examples of practical design. Scientists, engineers, and inventors look to nature for new ideas, products, and solutions to technical problems. One example concerns the Galápagos shark that is abundant worldwide around tropical oceanic islands. Its name results from detailed observation and study of the shark near the Galápagos Islands a century ago.

The Galápagos shark grows to 9.8 feet (3 meters) or longer. One unusual feature is that, while relatively slow moving, the shark's skin remains remarkably clear of barnacles, algae, and bacteria. In contrast, such passengers are common on the surface of other slow swimmers including whales. Close inspection of the shark skin reveals the root reason for its clean surface: overlapping diamond-shaped scales are covered with tiny ridges and bumps. This textured skin discourages the formation of bacteria growth. As a result, the shark skin remains clean and bacteria free.

Sharklet Technologies, Inc., has developed an adhesive film that mimics the bacterial resistant properties of Galápagos shark skin. The adhesive-backed vinyl film is embossed with a micro-pattern — a continuous pattern of diamond-shaped features designed to mimic shark scales. Tests show that the dimpled surface discourages the growth of harmful bacteria.

There are many valuable applications of the artificial shark skin product. For example, the hulls of ships often become fouled with bacterial films. The resulting frictional drag causes higher fuel cost amounting to millions of dollars annually for large vessels. Current efforts to combat underwater fouling often require paints containing heavy metals. Application of the artificial shark skin coating is found to give similar results without the use of these toxic metals.

Hospitals can be breeding grounds for unhealthy bacteria. As a precaution, the adhesive shark skin film can be applied to high-touch areas, including public restrooms, door handles, and medical instruments.

What is the origin of the Galápagos shark's ability to efficiently repel skin bacteria? The typical evolutionary response is that sharks and other creatures developed their own particular survival features during countless generations of slow change. Along the way, natural selection sorted out and preserved

the positive mutations. In this view, apparent design in nature is undirected and unplanned. Although popular, this view fails on several points.

First, the assumption of an evolutionary time scale is challenged by biblical and scientific data. "Deep time" is simply not available. Second, multiple positive mutations, such as those that led to the formation of the pattern on shark skin, are assumed to have occurred in the past, yet they are not observed in the present. Mutations are changes in the DNA that decrease the complexity and design of an

organism, not increase it. The popular notions of evolutionary change fail to account for this wonderful design of our wonderful Creator.

Nature is filled with near-endless examples of intelligent design. Even in a world that has fallen far from its perfect beginning, the fingerprints of the Creator are all around us. In the case of the Galápagos shark, we are taught a practical lesson for environmentally friendly bacteria control.

DON DEYOUNG

THE ECOSYSTEMS OF the Galápagos Islands are unique and, in keeping with the dominion mandate, efforts should be made to conserve them. One of the biggest threats to native animal and plant species are mammals introduced to the islands by man. Many of these mammals were once domesticated, such as dogs, pigs, and goats, but escaped human habitats and now live in the wild. They and their offspring are known as feral animals.

Feral animals can drastically change any ecosystem. Many times the changes include driving the native species to extinction. In the Galápagos, wild goats threaten some plant species. Pigs and dogs threaten the tortoises by consuming their eggs. Dogs and cats are also known to eat iguanas, penguins, and other birds. To protect the many rare and unique species of the islands, control measures are used to try to remove feral animals. This is often a long, difficult, and expensive process.

Pigs were probably introduced to Santiago Island in the 1800s soon after Darwin visited in 1835. Before the end of that century, they had become numerous and threatened a number of plant and animal species. It is believed that they were partly responsible for most of the extinctions of native animals on the islands. A program was initiated in 1968 to get rid of pigs. Two of the most successful methods used were hunting and poisoning. In addition, trails were cut to allow hunters easy access and intensive monitoring kept tabs on the progress. It took over 30 years to eradicate all the pigs on the island.

Similar methods were used to remove dogs. Shooting was not as effective when the island was large or there were large numbers of dogs. Some male dogs were chemically sterilized to prevent them from fathering puppies. Poisoning was found to be effective, but it was important to use a poison that would not affect species native to the island. A poison was used that was available in the country, relatively inexpensive, and would not normally be eaten by other animals in large enough quantities to kill them.

Similar methods were also used to remove feral goats. In the process it was found to be more effective to hunt by helicopter than on foot. To find the goats, sometimes a goat with a tracking device was released. Since goats like the company of other goats, the one with the tracking device naturally led the hunters to other goats on the island. Unfortunately, all the hard work of removing feral animals can be undone if people reintroduce them. To make these conservation efforts successful, people must be educated about the purpose of removing the feral animals to ensure that more are not released into the wild.

It is important to realize, however, that the dominion mandate does not imply that we must expend enormous time, energy, and resources to save every endangered species on the planet. The effort on the Galápagos affected numerous endangered species and involved cleaning up a mess that careless people had created. In addition, there is an effort to see that people who live locally are benefited by the management practices. For Christians, the well being of people, who were created in the image of God, must be the most important deciding factor as we attempt to follow the dominion mandate.

JEAN LIGHTNER

GENESIS 1:28 COMMANDS mankind to multiply, fill the earth, subdue it, and have dominion over it. It would be possible, taking them in isolation, to understand "subdue" and "have dominion" in a sense that could lead to abuse of the earth, but the wider teaching of Scripture makes that impossible. Rather, subduing and ruling the earth should mirror God's acts shown earlier in Genesis — a subduing and ruling that involves bringing increasing order, vitality, fruitfulness, and diversity to the earth as God did through His creative acts. That is, having been made in God's image, we are to rule as God rules — not abusively and destructively, but lovingly and creatively. And in the end, as the Parable of the Talents shows (Matthew 25:14–30), we are answerable to God for how we have done this. Therefore, the Church should be leading the way in proper stewardship of God's creation because we represent Him to each other and to His creation.

Romans 1:20 states, "For since the creation of the world His invisible attributes are clearly seen, being understood by the things that are made, even His eternal power and Godhead, so that they are without excuse." One of those attributes is His Trinitarian nature, and because of this quality, community and relationship are the foundation of His being. This passage teaches that we should see this quality in the physical creation, and we do. The study of ecology is the study of relationships and the more we understand diverse creatures and their relationships both with each other and the non-living world, the more we realize that health is rooted in community. Good stewards strive to carry out the dominion mandate and desire to understand not only complex human relationships, but also the complex relationships of our world. The more we understand, the better we can care for the things of God.

Because the Galápagos is so unique, there are many stewardship efforts that believers can support and endorse so that better care of the islands can be maintained and remediation from the harm done by human carelessness over the last couple of centuries can take place. Many conservation milestones have been reached in the past almost 80 years.

Frigate bird

YEAR	CONSERVATION MILESTONES
1936	Ecuador makes first laws to protect wildlife
1959	Galápagos National Park (97% of island surface area) and Charles Darwin Research Center established
1978	United Nations Educational, Scientific, and Cultural Organization recognizes as World Heritage Site
1984	Goals are set to improve man's relationship with environment through Man & Biosphere Program
1986	Galápagos Marine Resources Reserve created
1990	Galápagos Whale Sanctuary created
2001	Marine Resources Reserve designated as World Heritage Site
2005	International Maritime Organization declares Galápagos an area of Specially Sensitive Waters

Programs in the Galápagos focus on educating people who live on the islands on how to conserve the wonderful and unique environment in which they live.

The Center for Sustainable Life, as of 2007 and owned by the Nature Conservancy, had five major goals for residential areas on Santa Cruz: 1) garden organically, 2) develop local, natural crops, 3) restore damaged ecosystems, 4) generate ecotourism, and 5) provide jobs.

Many schools have an environmental education program as part of the regular curriculum. The Galapagaño teachers provide students with wonderful activities and ecological research in which students test hypotheses and provide real data about many of the unique and native creatures that are easily accessed from the classroom. The students learn important stewardship concepts from an early age.

Fabricio Valverde Environmental Park focuses on solid waste recycling, cleaning of coastal pollution, and stewardship education. For example, all paper, cardboard, and plastics are separated and shipped to the Ecuadorian mainland for recycling. Glass is ground up and made into paving stones like those used on the streets of Puerto Ayora, Santa Cruz. These efforts and many others have been successful in helping to restore the islands' unique and beautiful ecosystems.

TOM HENNIGAN

VISITING THE GALÁPAGOS Islands was for me a gift from God. It came right after I had lost my job as a ranger in an Arizona state park because of my belief in creation and refusal to teach school children visiting the park that the features there were millions or billions of years old. The Institute for Creation Research invited me to be guest lecturer on the birds of the Galápagos with a tour group. Our Ecuadorian tour guide was intrigued with our lectures on creation and a young earth, and I had the wonderful privilege of opening the Scriptures several times with him, showing him God's plan of salvation. Before our tour ended, he made a profession of faith in Christ. Praise be to our awesome God who "does great things past finding out, yes, wonders without number" (Job 9:10).

DONNA O'DANIEL

THERE WAS ONE truly unique experience when I visited the Galápagos Islands — moving freely among wild animals that did not fear me. Sharing that experience with my ancestors who lived before the Flood (Genesis 2:19) impressed on me even more that a straightforward reading of Genesis is true and can be trusted.

ROGER SANDERS

THE MYSTERIOUS BEAUTY of the Galápagos archipelago came into view as we approached the Baltra runway. Was I just imagining or was my life-long dream of visiting these islands actually about to begin? As I explored these lands, heralded as the Mecca for evolutionary naturalists, it was obvious to me that these islands instead powerfully reflect the Creator's attributes of beauty, design, provision, and sustainment in a fallen and imperfect world. Each day brought renewed experiences of worship, joy, and thankfulness as I reflected on being in the company of creatures that showed no fear.

I sat among marine iguanas as they went about their daily feeding and sunbathing rituals. I walked with giant tortoises as they grazed upon their mid-day meal. I snorkeled with sea lions that wanted to play. I ate with Darwin's finches that desired to share my food. It seemed that God wanted me to glimpse Adam's world before the Fall and embrace the hope that His children look forward to when Christ makes all things new and creation is at peace. I will never forget my time in those mysterious lands because it was there that Christ gave me a glimpse into both himself and the promises He has made for those who love Him and who are called according to His purposes.

TOM HENNIGAN

87

OVER 45 YEARS of teaching science, we have seen more and more of God's creative genius in creation and wanted to show our students the biblical perspective of the origin of life. Every secular science textbook hails Darwin as the god of this age, ascribing to him the answers about the origin of life. We want our students and future generations to know the truth about his so-called discoveries.

So the one place we had to visit was the Galápagos Islands. Why? To point out that the geological and biological evidence in the present (observational science) confirms the creation and Flood accounts in Genesis chapters 1–11, as well as the scientific models we develop to understand those events (historical science).

We wanted to see for ourselves the same evidence observed by Darwin that eventually led him to propose that all living things descended from a common ancestor. We wanted to show our students the importance of worldview when it comes to observing the present and its relation to the past. We wanted our students to see the intricate details of God's amazing creation first hand.

We climbed the Prince Phillip Steps to traverse the rim of Isla Genovesa amid thousands of birds, stood among the giant Galápagos tortoises just minutes away from the Darwin Research Station, trekked up the side of Sierra Negra to view the second–largest active volcanic crater in the world, wandered among the blue-footed boobies, watched the sea lions play alongside our inflatable boat, laughed at the marine iguanas sneezing excess salt from their bodies, and enjoyed discussions after dinner describing the fingerprints of God we had seen that day.

As we explored different islands, we discussed the need to reduce alien species of plants and animals that harm the native populations. Our students understood God created a robust world, not a fragile world, and our duty remains to manage its fauna and flora responsibly.

After days of observing the beauty and complexity of the islands, we wanted our students to be able to respond with the same awe as the Psalmist in Psalm 95:3: "For the LORD is the great God, and the great King above all gods."

Did we achieve our objective? We believe we did. We all returned with a more vibrant faith in the simple facts of creation: God did what He said He did. It's that simple. And we believe Him!

LANCE AND PENNEY DAVIS

Blue-footed booby courtship ritual

He shakes the earth out of its place,
And its pillars tremble;
—Job 9:6

BEFORE I VISITED them, the Galápagos Islands had always seemed such a mysterious place — mystical and enticing. The folklore that had grown up around Darwin's visit implied to me a lush rainforest environment. Much to my surprise, the islands are essentially made up of barren volcanic rock, although swarming with exotic life. Giant tortoises are there, as are marine iguanas, diving frigate birds, and finches — a great variety of finches. These helped make the original case for Darwin's theory of evolution by natural selection, giving the Galápagos enormous scientific significance. Many secular scientists, who start with man's ideas about the past and deny God's influence, think these islands "prove" geological and biological evolution.

Creation scientists have a different understanding and interpretation of the evidence on the islands. The Bible is our starting point for developing models to understand how the islands formed, how life migrated to the islands, and how life adapted to the islands. Because of our different starting point, we come to different conclusions than secular scientists concerning the past and the present.

Few locations on earth are as conducive to good observation as the Galápagos. The animals are abundant and remarkably unafraid of humans. Restriction on human activity protects both them and their habitat, allowing good observations to be made. Unfortunately, scientists who have chosen to start with man's ideas about the past apart from God have a wrong bias that has produced blindness to the truth. The only correct bias is the Word of God because God is an eyewitness to the past.

Wearing biblical "glasses," an observer can properly understand the evidence in the present and conclude that observational science confirms clear biblical teachings about the past and the models we develop to understand them better (historical science). Observational science, however, clearly contradicts the historical science of geological and biological evolution.

JOHN MORRIS

91

CONCLUSION

When I was asked to travel with a group of Atlanta homeschool students to the Galápagos Islands, my first thought was sheer bliss. This is every biologist's dream come true! My second thought was sheer agony. I realized I would be separated from my young daughter, Elizabeth, for more than two weeks. We are very close, and I wasn't sure how either of us would handle the separation.

Friends, family, and coworkers encouraged me to go. After all, it was an opportunity of a lifetime. I finally agreed, reminded myself that my family was in God's hands, and went to the Galápagos. As it turned out, when I could get a cell phone signal and would call home, Elizabeth was fine. Dad and Grandma kept her busy, and before I knew it, we were back together again.

It wasn't until after I returned that the importance of this trip began to sink in. I shared with my daughter the pictures and videos and told her all about the amazing animals and landscapes I had witnessed. I shared with her the biblical perspective of how the Galápagos Islands formed and life colonized the islands. One of the most important ministries I have on earth is training Elizabeth to love God, trust His Word, and equip her with answers for this skeptical age.

I don't know if or what Darwin told his children about his adventures in the Galápagos Islands. If he did, I'm sure that his accounts of their origins were very different from mine. How is this possible? Both Darwin and I watched enormous Galápagos tortoises munch on vegetation. We both marveled at the ability of marine iguanas to dive into the chilly water for food. We both saw blue-footed boobies, finches, and mockingbirds. And we both witnessed barren landscapes that resulted from large volcanic eruptions.

Darwin and I viewed the same evidence yet interpreted it differently due to our different starting points. Again, how the islands formed and were colonized falls under the category of historical (or origins) science. This type of scientific inquiry is very dependent on a person's worldview. Darwin believed his ideas about the past (including millions of years and the common ancestry of all living things) were correct and God's Word was wrong. I believe that the eyewitness account of God recorded in Genesis — the inerrant Word of God — is correct, and man's ideas about the past apart from God are wrong.

The scientists in this book have shown that observational (or operational) science in relation to the Galápagos Islands confirms and is consistent with God's Word. It is inconsistent with and does not confirm evolutionary ideas, including millions of years. Although we don't need something outside of Scripture to prove its truthfulness, we expect what we observe in the world to be consistent with God's Word . . . and it is.

In the introduction to this book, I shared a passage from Job 12 in which Job says that nature itself can teach us about God. The knowledge of God from nature is called general revelation. In a later section in the Book of Job, God Himself uses His creation to help Job see that the all-knowing, all-powerful God is in complete control and nothing happens outside of His plans and purposes (Job 38–41).

Then the LORD answered Job out of the whirlwind, and said:
"Who is this who darkens counsel
By words without knowledge?
Now prepare yourself like a man;
I will question you, and you shall answer Me"

—Job 38:1–3

A few chapters later Job humbly answers God and says,

I know that You can do everything,
And that no purpose of Yours can be withheld from You.
You asked, "Who is this who hides counsel without knowledge?"
Therefore I have uttered what I did not understand,
Things too wonderful for me, which I did not know.

—Job 42:2–3

God is not elevating nature above special revelation, His written Word, but showing Job that only He has a perfect understanding of nature because He is the Creator God. As the Apostle Paul points out, the whole of creation is groaning under the weight of the curse God placed on it after Adam sinned (Romans 8:20–22). Nature is corrupted by sin (the Fall of man recorded in Genesis 3) and so it can never be a perfect reflection of God. Theologian Louis Berkhof said, "Since the entrance of sin into the world, man can gather true knowledge about God from His general revelation only if he studies it in the light of Scripture."[1] The creation we are studying has been corrupted by sin, and we cannot understand it rightly apart from acknowledging its broken condition.

Sadly, many Christians have tried to incorporate man's ideas about the past apart from God (the old-earth concepts of evolution and millions of years of history) into Genesis chapters 1 and 2. They believe these ideas only affect how we read and understand Genesis, but this simply isn't true. These ideas impugn the very nature of God. In this view, fossils and rock layers are records of millions of years of suffering and death rather than the result of catastrophic processes just thousands of years ago. If God used evolutionary processes over millions of years to eventually bring about man, then this means that He called death, disease, and struggle — all necessary components to the old-age view — "very good" when He was finished creating (Genesis 1:31).

Yet death is the punishment for sin (Genesis 2–3; Romans 6:23); hardly a "good" thing. And Paul called death the "last enemy" (1 Corinthians 15:26). If death is "very good," then the Bible passages that follow Genesis 1 are wrong, and to put it bluntly, God is a sadist. He can hardly be the just and merciful God showcased in the rest of the Bible — the God who sent His Son to save us from the deadly and eternal effects of sin.

In fact, the basis for the good news that Jesus Christ came into the world to save us from our own rebellion,

1   Louis Berkhof, *Systematic Theology* (Grand Rapids, MI: Wm. B. Eerdmans, 1996), p. 96.

a rebellion that started with Adam disobeying God in the Garden of Eden, is undermined when the historicity of Genesis is denied or compromised. If Adam was not a real person who sinned against God, and if we are not all really his descendants who have inherited his sinful nature, choosing to disobey God and placing ourselves under the punishment of death (Romans 5:12), then why did the God-Man, Jesus Christ, come to earth and suffer and die on the Cross (John 3:16–17)? The Apostle Paul made clear the foundational importance of the actions of the first, real, historical Adam to the actions of the last, real, historical Adam — Jesus Christ,

> For as in Adam all die, even so in Christ all shall be made alive.
>
> —1 Corinthians 15:22

> And so it is written, "The first man Adam became a living being." The last Adam became a life-giving spirit.
>
> —1 Corinthians 15:45

From carefully studying the entire counsel of Scripture, we can be certain that God didn't use evolution and millions of years and that He is loving, just, and merciful. It is also clear that we all disobey God's commands and are deserving of death and eternal separation from God forever in hell. If you don't think this description fits you, stop and examine yourself in the light of the Ten Commandments (Exodus 20:1–17) or in light of the perfect obedience of Jesus Christ to all of those commands (2 Corinthians 5:20–21). If you are honest, you will acknowledge your own sin and the perfection of Jesus. But just as God was merciful to Noah and his family in providing an ark for their physical salvation from the watery judgment, God provides spiritual salvation through the Redeemer, His Son, Jesus Christ.

Although Jesus was sinless (Hebrews 4:15), He took the sin of all mankind (1 Peter 2:24) and the wrath of God for that sin on Himself (1 Thessalonians 5:9). He took the punishment that was ours and died a horrific death on the Cross (Romans 5:6–8). The good news is that He didn't stay dead; He resurrected and returned to heaven (1 Corinthians 15:3–4)! His death made it possible for us to be forgiven of our sins, to have a restored relationship with God, and to live eternally in heaven with Him when we repent of our sins and place our trust in Christ for the forgiveness He offers (Acts 20:20–21; Romans 10:9).

The Galápagos Islands are an awesome display of God's majesty and mercy. I hope this book has challenged you to recognize the importance of starting points when it comes to understanding the past and the impact it has on the present. Truth can only be found when we start with God's Word.

In His hand are the deep places of the earth;
the heights of the hills are His also.

—Psalm 95:4

John Baumgardner, PhD, Geophysics and Space Physics

He has a BS in electrical engineering from Texas Tech University, an MS in electrical engineering from Princeton University, and an MS and PhD in geophysics and space physics from UCLA. Baumgardner is a contributor to the concept of catastrophic plate tectonics as an important aspect of the Genesis Flood; a member of the Radioisotopes and the Age of the Earth (RATE) research team; and a member of the development team of Mendel's Accountant, a computer model for population genetics. He is currently vice president and senior research associate of Logos Research Associates in Santa Ana, California.

Lance Davis, Co-Founder, Living Science

Born and raised in Zimbabwe, Davis graduated from the Rhodesia Teachers' College in 1963 and taught in schools, rising to the position of assistant principal. He took graduate classes at Capital Bible Seminary, Lanham, Maryland, before returning to Zimbabwe as a missionary. Davis immigrated to the USA in 1979 and co-founded Living Science for homeschoolers in 1996. He helped design the unique format for learning at Living Science, including hands-on classes, engineering, and technology emphasis expeditions, with a focus on ecology and marine biology and servant leader training for high school students.

Penney Davis, Co-Founder, Living Science

Born in South Africa, Davis was raised in Zimbabwe and graduated from the Rhodesia Teachers' College with a major in science and education. After immigrating to the USA in 1979, she taught in schools in New York, and became the science "kit" coordinator for BOCES in New York state. She supplied teachers in multiple counties with training and science equipment. Davis was science department head at a Christian school in Georgia before starting Living Science with her husband in 1996. She has successfully led hands-on expeditions to many different marine venues in the South, teaching young-earth creation as a basis for science education. Davis has also conducted continuing education classes for teachers in the subjects of "learning styles" and hands-on science education.

Don DeYoung, PhD, Solid State Physics

He has a BS in applied physics, an MS in solid state physics from Michigan Tech University, an MDiv from Grace Theological Seminary, and a PhD in solid state physics from Iowa State University. As chair of the Science and Mathematics Department at Grace College in Winona Lake, Indiana, and president of the Creation Research Society, DeYoung is well-known in apologetics circles, having written 20 books as well as 400 articles and book reviews.

Danny Faulkner, PhD, Astronomy

He has a BS in math from Bob Jones University, an MS in physics from Clemson University, and an MA and PhD in astronomy from Indiana University, Faulkner is a research scientist, speaker, and writer for Answers in Genesis. He is also the author of *Universe by Design*, and is a Distinguished Professor Emeritus at University of South Carolina-Lancaster.

Ken Ham, President and CEO, Answers in Genesis and the Creation Museum

He has a B. App. Sc. in biology from Queensland Institute of Technology and a Dip. Ed. in general science from University of Queensland. As the author of numerous books and articles on biblical authority and creation, including *The Lie: Evolution/Millions of Years,* Ham hosts a daily radio program called Answers, and is an internationally known speaker on the topic of biblical authority and creation.

Steve Ham, MDiv

He has a CFP in finance from Deakin University (Melbourne) and is currently working on an MDiv at Southern Baptist Theological Seminary. Ham serves as senior director of outreach for Answers in Genesis and is also the author of *In God We Trust* and a contributor to *How Do We Know the Bible Is True, Vol. 1*.

Tom Hennigan, MS, Education and MPS, Environmental and Forest Biology

He has a BS in natural resources management from the University of Alaska, Fairbanks, an MS in education from Syracuse University, and an MPS in environmental and forest biology from the State University of New York College of Environmental Science and Forestry. Hennigan is co-author of *The Ecology Book* (Wonders of Creation Series), serves as a researcher on the ark kinds research team for Answers in Genesis' Ark Encounter, and won the Outstanding Science Teacher Award from the Technology Club of Syracuse. Currently he is an associate professor of biology at Truett-McConnell College.

Nathaniel Jeanson, PhD, Cell and Developmental Biology

He has a BS in molecular biology and bioinformatics from the University of Wisconsin at Parkside and a PhD from Harvard University in cell and developmental biology. Jeanson is currently deputy director for Life Sciences Research at the Institute for Creation Research. He is known for his work in studying the role of vitamin D in adult blood stem cell regulation and with the Bio-Origins Project to understand the origin of species from a biblical perspective.

Jean Lightner, DVM

She has a BS in agriculture majoring in animal science, an MS in veterinary preventive medicine, and a DVM all from The Ohio State University. Lightner actively researches and publishes in the area of creation biology, serves as a researcher on the ark kinds research team for Answers in Genesis' Ark Encounter, and is currently an adjunct instructor for Liberty University Online, in addition to being an independent researcher.

Jason Lisle, PhD, Astrophysics

He has a BA in physics and astronomy from Ohio Wesleyan University and an MS and PhD in astrophysics from the University of Colorado at Boulder in the field of solar supergranulation. Lisle discovered polar alignments of supergranules and giant cell boundaries, is the author of several books on creation astronomy and presuppositional apologetics, and currently serves as director of research at the Institute for Creation Research.

Tommy Mitchell, MD

He has a BA in cell biology from the University of Tennessee, Knoxville and an MD from Vanderbilt University School of Medicine. Mitchell was elected Fellow of the American College of Physicians in 1991 and now serves as a speaker and writer for Answers in Genesis.

John Morris, PhD, Geological Engineering

He has a BS in civil engineering from Virginia Polytechnic Institute and an MS and PhD in geological engineering from the University of Oklahoma. As a former assistant professor at the university, as well as related to his research in the areas of coal mining and technology, Morris has written a number of articles and books related to creation, age of the earth, fossils, the Flood, and the search for Noah's ark. He is currently the president for the Institute for Creation Research.

Terry Mortenson, PhD, History of Geology

He has a BA in math from the University of Minnesota, an MDiv from Trinity Evangelical Divinity School in Deerfield, Illinois, and a PhD in the history of geology from Coventry University in England. As a speaker, writer, and researcher with Answers in Genesis, Mortenson is well known for his extensive research related to the history of geology. He authored *The Great Turning Point: The Church's Catastrophic Mistake on Geology — Before Darwin,* and served as both a co-editor and contributing writer for *Coming to Grips with Genesis: Biblical Authority and the Age of the Earth.*

Donna O'Daniel, MA, Biological Sciences

She has a BA in bible and Christian education from Faith Baptist Bible College in Ankeny, Iowa, and an MA in biological sciences from the University of Texas at Austin. O'Daniel has worked as a biologist in Alaska, NW Hawaiian Islands, and Johnston Atoll on seabirds; Northern Marianas on five endangered species, and on Madagascar for the endangered Madagascar fish eagle. She is an ornithologist and has been a lecturer on three Pacific Ocean cruises, and one each to Antarctica and the Galápagos Islands. O'Daniel co-authored two species accounts in the *Birds of North America* series and completed a two-year, first-ever breeding biology study of Bulwer's Petrel.

Michael Oard, MS, Atmospheric Science

He has a BS and MS in atmospheric science from the University of Washington. Oard was a research meteorologist for six years at the University of Washington and has published several research articles in journals and technical monographs of the American Meteorological Society. Oard retired in 2001 after 30 years of service in the National Weather Service and does full-time research, writing, and speaking in creation earth science. He has also authored, coauthored, or been editor of 17 creation books and has published over 200 articles in creation technical literature.

Doug Oliver, PhD, Ecology

He has a BS in biology and an MS in zoology from the University of Toronto on effects of a proposed nuclear reactor on bass in one of the Great Lakes; and a PhD in ecology from the University of Georgia, on fish ecology of Okefenokee Swamp. Oliver has published environmental and creation science articles and worked as a State of Florida biologist and environmental manager (while also teaching part-time at Florida A & M University for several years). In addition, he has worked for environmental consulting companies and as a biology professor at Liberty University.

Gary Parker, EdD, Biology and Geology

He has a BA in biology and chemistry from Wabash College and an MS and EdD with a focus in biology and geology from Ball State University. Having founded three college biology departments, published 17 books, and participated in many creation debates, Parker is now director of the Creation Adventures Museum, Florida, and a lecturer with Answers in Genesis.

Roger Patterson, BSed, Biology

He has a BSed (Bachelor of Science Education) in biology from Montana State University-Billings. Patterson is a curriculum writer for Answers in Genesis. He is the author of *Evolution Exposed: Biology* and *Evolution Exposed: Earth Science,* as well as being a member of the writing team for Answers Bible Curriculum.

Georgia Purdom, PhD, Molecular Genetics

She has a BA in biology from Cedarville University and a PhD in molecular genetics from The Ohio State University. Purdom is the author of numerous articles and book chapters in the field of creation biology and has published several research articles in *Answers Research Journal* and *Proceedings of the International Conference on Creationism.* She also served as a biology professor for six years at Mount Vernon Nazarene University. Purdom is currently a researcher, speaker, and writer for Answers in Genesis.

Ron Samec, PhD, Physics

He has a BA in astronomy, an MA in science education with a focus in physics from the University of South Florida, and a PhD in physics from Clemson University. Currently working as professor of physics and astronomy at Bob Jones University, among Samec's notable works are "On the Origin of Lunar Maria," *Journal of Creation* and "BVRcIc Observations and Analyses of the Dwarf Detached Binary V1043 Cassiopeia and a Comment on Precontact W UMa's," *The Astronomical Journal,* and 183 articles referenced on the SAO/NASA Astrophysical Data System.

Roger Sanders, PhD, Systematic Botany

He has a BA in biology from College of the Ozarks and a PhD in systematic botany from the University of Texas at Austin. Sanders is on faculty at Core Academy of Science. His work includes determining the origin of rosette trees of Juan Fernández Islands in Chile and taxonomy of *Lantana*.

Frank Sherwin, MA, Zoology

He has a BA in biology from Western State College and an MA in zoology with a focus in parasitology from the University of Northern Colorado. Sherwin is an active speaker, science writer, and author with the Institute for Creation Research. Some of his most significant work is related to the role of parasites in the biblical Fall and Curse.

Andrew Snelling, PhD, Geology

He has a BSc (Hons) from the University of New South Wales in Sydney, Australia, and a PhD in geology from the University of Sydney. Snelling is director of research at Answers in Genesis. He also served as principal investigator and editor of the RATE project; authored *Earth's Catastrophic Past;* took part in the Cataclysmic Chronology Research Group; and served as editor and contributor to *Grappling with the Chronology of the Genesis Flood* (in press).

Jeffrey Tomkins, PhD, Genetics

He has a BS in agriculture education majoring in horticulture from Washington State University, an MS in plant science physiology from the University of Idaho, and a PhD in genetics from Clemson University. With over 80 journal publications and book chapters in the field of genomics and genetics as well as having published two books, Tomkins is a research scientist in genomics and genetics with the Institute for Creation Research.

Larry Vardiman, PhD, Atmospheric Science

He has a BS in physics from the University of Missouri at Rolla, a BS in meteorology from St. Louis University, and an MS and PhD in atmospheric science from Colorado State University. Vardiman has done significant work in the fields of cloud physics and weather modification.

John C. Whitcomb, ThD, Old Testament

He has an AB in history (with honors) from Princeton University, a BDiv (now MDiv), ThM, and ThD in Old Testament from Grace Theological Seminary. Whitcomb co-authored *The Genesis Flood* with the late Dr. Henry Morris in 1961, a work that has been credited as one of the major catalysts for the modern biblical creationism movement. Whitcomb is heard weekly as the Bible teacher on *Encounter God's Truth,* a new radio and Internet broadcast outreach of Whitcomb Ministries, Inc. He has been a professor of Old Testament and theology for 60 years and is widely recognized as a leading biblical scholar. He is president of Whitcomb Ministries, Inc.

John Whitmore, PhD, Biology (Paleontology)

He has a BS in geology from Kent State University, an MS in geology from the Institute for Creation Research, and a PhD in biology with an emphasis in paleontology specifically fish taphonomy and sedimentology from Loma Linda University. Currently working at Cedarville University, as professor of geology, Whitmore is noted for his work in the study of Coconino Sandstone in the Grand Canyon.

Gordon Wilson, PhD, Environmental Science and Public Policy

He has a BS in secondary education/biological sciences, MS in entomology from the University of Idaho, and a PhD in environmental science and public policy with a research emphasis in herpetology from George Mason University. He has written and published a couple articles on the reproductive ecology of the eastern box turtle and is currently Senior Fellow of Natural History at New Saint Andrews College.

Todd Charles Wood, PhD, Biochemistry

He has a BS in biology from Liberty University and a PhD in biochemistry from the University of Virginia. Wood is president of Core Academy of Science. He has worked for 14 years in the area of statistical baraminology trying to identify created kinds from statistical data.

REFERENCES

Books

DeYoung, Don. *Thousands . . . Not Billions*. Green Forest, AR: Master Books, 2005.

DeYoung, Don, and Derrik Hobbs. *Discovery of Design*. Green Forest, AR: Master Books, 2010.

Ham, Ken. *The Lie*. Green Forest, AR: Master Books, 2012.

Ham, Ken (ed.). *The New Answers Book 1*. Green Forest, AR: Master Books, 2006.

Lightner, Jean, and Tom Hennigan. *The Ecology Book*. Green Forest, AR: Master Books, 2013.

Lisle, Jason. *The Ultimate Proof*. Green Forest, AR: Master Books: 2009.

Lisle, Jason. *The Stargazer's Guide to the Night Sky*. Green Forest, AR: Master Books, 2012.

Morris, Henry M., and John W. Whitcomb. **The Genesis Flood*. Phillipsburg, NJ: P&R Publishing, 2011. *Editor's note: This classic work, which launched the modern creationist revolution, first appeared in 1961 and therefore some of the geological material in this book may be considered outdated. But the overall framework remains foundational in the thinking of creationist scientists worldwide.

Morris, John. *The Geology Book*. Green Forest, AR: Master Books, 2000.

Morris, John. *The Global Flood.* Dallas, TX: ICR, 2012.

Mortenson, Terry and Thane H. Ury, (eds.). *Coming to Grips with Genesis.* Green Forest, AR: Master Books, 2008.

Oard, Michael. *The Weather Book.* Green Forest, AR: Master Books, 1997.

Parker, Gary. *Creation Facts of Life.* Green Forest, AR: Master Books, 2006.

Patterson, Roger. *Evolution Exposed: Biology.* Green Forest, AR: Master Books, 2006.

Patterson, Roger. *Evolution Exposed: Earth Science.* Green Forest, AR: Master Books, 2008.

Sherwin, Frank. *The Ocean Book.* Green Forest, AR: Master Books, 2004.

Snelling, Andrew. *Earth's Catastrophic Past* (Volumes 1 and 2). Dallas, TX: ICR, 2010.

Wood, Todd C. *A Creationist Review and Preliminary Analysis of the History, Geology, Climate, and Biology of the Galápagos Islands.* Center for Origins Research, Issues in Creation No. 1, Eugene, OR: Wipf and Stock Pub., 2005.

Articles

Hennigan, T., G. Purdom, T.C. Wood, "Creation's Hidden Potential," *Answers Magazine* (Jan.–March 2009): 70–75, http://www.answersingenesis.org/articles/am/v4/n1/hidden-potential.

Mitchell, Mary, "Salt Sneezing Lizards," *Answers Magazine* (Jan.–March 2009): 20, http://www.answersingenesis.org/articles/am/v4/n1/salt-sneezing-lizards.

Morris, John, "Galápagos: Showcase for Creation," *Acts & Facts* 38(5) (2009): 8, http://www.icr.org/article/galapagos-showcase-for-creation/.

Purdom, Georgia, " 'Evolution' of Finch Beaks — Again" (2006), http://www.answersingenesis.org/articles/aid/v1/n1/evolution-finch-beaks-again.

Sanders, R., "Finding God in Galápagos," *Answers Magazine* (Jan–March 2009): 40–45, http://www.answersingenesis.org/articles/am/v4/n1/galapagos.

Thomas, Brian, "Rediscovered 'Extinct' Tortoise Frustrates Darwinism" (2012), http://www.icr.org/article/rediscovered-extinct-tortoise-frustrates/.

Thomas, Brian, "New Finch Species Shows Conservation, Not Macroevolution" (2009), http://www.icr.org/article/5118/.

DVDs

The Mysterious Islands, Vision Forum, 2009

The Evolution of Darwin, Answers in Genesis, 2009

Websites

Answers in Genesis — www.answersingenesis.org

Institute for Creation Research — www.icr.org

Creation Research Society — www.crs.org

Creation Biology Society — www.creationbiology.org

Dr. John W. Whitcomb — www.whitcombministries.org

101

Whether gaping at the huge chasm in the earth from the rim, or navigating the waters of the Colorado River below, visitors to the Grand Canyon see a perspective that words can't describe. In fact, perspective is the backdrop for this wonderful story from nature. Visit this marvelous site yourself through the pages of photographs and essays in this book, and think about your own perspective. It's a trip you'll be glad you took.

GRAND CANYON

a different view

written and compiled by Tom Vail

978-0-89051-373-6 | $16.99

GRAND CANYON
A DIFFERENT VIEW

The Grand Canyon is an awesome display of God's creation. Carved through layers of limestone, sandstone, shale, schist, and granite, this great chasm stretches 277 miles through the Colorado Plateau. It descends over a mile into the earth and extends as much as 18 miles in width. The Canyon holds within its walls mountains that are taller than anything east of the Mississippi River. Grand Canyon National Park encompasses both Marble Canyon and Grand Canyon.

The Grand Canyon is also a place to find and explore the wonders of His creation. When viewed from a biblical perspective, the Canyon has "God" written all over it, from the splendor and grandeur of the Canyon walls, to the intelligent design of the Creator displayed in the creatures that inhabit this magical place.

Not only is the Canyon a testimony to creation, but it also presents evidence of God's judgment of the world, as told in the book of Genesis. It was a judgment by water of a world broken by the sin of man known as "the Fall." (See the Genesis account of the Days of Creation, the Fall, and the Flood on pages 10-11.) The Canyon gives us a glimpse of the effects of a catastrophic global flood, as well as an appreciation for the scale of the biblical Flood of Noah's day. And at the same time, we see God's handiwork in the beauty and majesty of the earth that we live in today.

Visitors to the Grand Canyon generally find it to be awe inspiring, but at the same time, too overwhelming to be fully understood on its own, for the Canyon can't tell us about itself. As humans, we tend to ask two questions as we view this vast, mysterious hole in the ground: how and why. With the help of some of the top creation scientists and theologians from around the world, we hope to at least scratch the surface of these questions and provide you with some resources to "dig deeper" if you wish.

If we visit the Canyon, or read the prevailing interpretive literature about it, we will find that the views presented are predominantly based on evolutionary theories. For the Canyon, this means that the rock layers were laid down a particle at a time over literally hundreds of millions of years and that the Canyon was later carved slowly by the Colorado River. These theories tend to deny God's involvement and often His very existence.

As you read this book, you will see that we look at the Canyon from a biblical worldview. With that in mind, there is one basic premise, or framework, used as a starting point. That premise is: the Bible, in its original form, is the inerrant Word of God.

Therefore, there are three truths that should be clarified. First, in Genesis a "day" is a day, which means a literal 24-hour period of time (technically a "solar day" which is approximately 24 hours). Genesis 1:5 says "... And there was evening and there was morning, one day." Second, there was no death before sin. The first death came as a result of initial

(Left) The tranquil falls of Elves Chasm

(Bottom Left) Desert bighorn sheep, common visitors to the Canyon's depths

(Below) Chuckwallas can reach 16 inches in length.

Marble Canyon